INTENTIONAL STEPS

The Pathway to Better Living

DR. STEVEN A. JIRGAL

CORE

Copyright © 2019 by Dr. Steven A. Jirgal

All rights reserved. No part of this publication may be reproduced, stored in a retrieval system, or transmitted in any form or by any means — electronic, mechanical, photocopy, recording, or any other — except for brief quotation in printed reviews, without the prior written permission of the publisher.

Unless otherwise indicated, Scripture quotations in this book are taken from the *New American Standard Bible*®, Copyright © 1960, 1962, 1963, 1968, 1971, 1972, 1973, 1975, 1977, 1995 by The Lockman Foundation. Used by permission.

Published by The Core Media Group, Inc., P.O. Box 2037, Indian Trail, NC 28079.

Printed in the United States of America.

Table of Contents

Introduction 5

1-Steps To Gaining Greater Wisdom 7

2-Steps To Developing A Winning Attitude 15

3-Steps To A Richer Marriage 25

4-Steps To Academic Growth 33

5-Steps To Experiencing Financial Success 39

6-Steps To Effective Parenting 45

7-Steps To Athletic Successs 53

8-Steps To Fulfilling Worship 59

9-Steps To Establishing An Overcomer's Life 65

10-Steps To Building A Hall Of Fame Life 73

Conclusion 83

Introduction

It is said that life's greatest journey begins with a single step. With the truth of that idea, this book is written. Along your journey of life, there is much to be seen, experienced and gathered. Each of us is a product of our past. Our lives are shaped by that which we see, the people we encounter, and the experiences we've have. With that in mind, we understand that it is possible to shape our future by adjusting our present. Life can be better tomorrow because of the decisions we make today.

This is seen is the illustration of a conversation a man had with his daughter. Katie was a twenty-four-year-old woman who was struggling with several issues in her life. One evening she was complaining to her father about how tough life was becoming. She was frustrated at work, disappointed with her friends, and angry at her boyfriend.

Her father listened patiently without interrupting. As Katie continued to spew out her frustrations, he quietly placed three pots filled with water on the stove. Into one of the pots he placed a couple of fresh carrots. Into another, he dropped a raw egg. In the third, he poured coffee grinds. Then he set all three pots to boiling.

After a while, his daughter asked him what he was doing. He explained, "Each of these three pots represents the struggles in life that are common to us all. And each of the items in the pots shows what our reaction to the struggles can be. The choice is ours."

Then he removed each of the items and placed them on the counter. "When difficulties come, we can be like the carrot and become soft and mushy." Then pointing to the egg, he said, "Or we can be like the egg and be hardened completely through." Lastly, he waved his hand above the pot containing the coffee grinds. "Or we can be like the coffee grinds and change the water we are in. We can't choose our struggles, but we can always choose our reaction to the difficulties that come our way."

Life is literally filled with choices. Some of the choices we have are non-consequential. Others can be life-changing. The key is to recognize those that carry great weight and those that are of little affect.

Intentional Steps deals with the issues that are paramount in our lives. Seeking wisdom, learning to be a good student, developing a positive attitude, pouring into your marriage, and other topics are essential to going to the next level in life and growing to your full potential. Take the following intentional step in your life and enjoy the journey!

- 1 -
Steps to Gaining Greater Wisdom

Everyone desires to be wise. Who wouldn't? But few really understand what true wisdom is and how to attain it. Wisdom is not the same as knowledge. Knowledge is simply the gathering of facts. Wisdom, however, is the gathering of those facts and applying them at the proper time and to the proper place. People with knowledge know that the Titanic struck an ice-burg and sank on April 15, 1912. They can tell you the time and cause of the loss of the vessel. They may even be able to tell you how many people lost their lives. But a wise person is the one who is on the ship and alerts the captain to the impending danger. He knows facts and is able to apply them to the situation thereby averting disaster.

Regarding the functional side of information, you will find that people can be categorized into one of three areas:

A-Fools: A fool is one who makes a mistake but does not learn from it. Thus, he is destined to repeat that same mistake over and over again. Fools can be easily identified. They seem to be always bruised, broke, and blaming. Physically, they keep hurting themselves by doing the same things and participating in the same activity. They get into fights because they haven't learned the art of tact, discretion, and restraint. They don't take proper safety precautions because they don't believe the laws of physics apply to them. Financially, they get paid on Friday and are broke on Monday because once again they've wasted their time and money on weekend indulgences. Socially, they never see themselves as the causation of their troubles. It always seems to be the other guy's fault for the accident, the forgetfulness, and the price of repairs.

B-Smart People: These are the ones who make mistakes but learn from them and are able to avoid them in the future. A majority of people you know fall into this category. They look at situations and harken back to similar situations remembering the outcome. If the outcome was positive, they try to replicate the decision and repeat the positive results. If the outcome was negative, they make the proper adjustments and side-step the bad results. This is a positive approach to situations but does carry with it a minor flaw. A smart person learns from *their* mistakes. That means that they must encounter numerous situations and circumstances and file them away for future reference. This can become very cumbersome.

C-Wise People: A wise person is not without their own mistakes. But one of the great benefits of being wise is, a wise person doesn't have to make mistakes in order to gain the benefit of experience. He can see the results of others' actions and learn from their decisions and mistakes. He side-steps problems and learns from mistakes-the mistakes of others!

Good news! You don't have to be a fool and you can go past the level of being smart. You can become a wise person-a person known for your wisdom. Following are ten principles that will guide you into wisdom and bring you to the coveted third category.

1-Become an Expert at Something

Find something that you have a keen interest in and focus on learning all you can about it. A curious mind gains knowledge and experience. This will take time and energy (and perhaps money), but the investment required to gain this knowledge will be well worth it. This means that you must learn to listen when you would rather talk. Larry King once said, "I've never learned anything while talking." This is sound insight. Those who would gain knowledge must learn the fine art of listening with the intent of learning. This means that you must approach people (even when it's uncomfortable) and listen to their insight borne from experience. There is a wealth of wisdom to be had simply by pursuing the company of those who are wise.

You must also spend time reading and investigating the subject. This is not easy and can take a lot of time, but you must commit to picking up material that can be added to your knowledge on a particular subject.

2-Surround Yourself with Wise People

The people you let into your life determine the way you go out in life. What you will find is that you become what you surround yourself with. If you're an athlete and you spend your time with other athletes who want to improve, you will find yourself becoming a better athlete. As a student, you'll become a better student when you spend time with good students. Running in the circles of those who have marriages that have failed bringing bitterness into their lives is not the path to improving your marriage. You must connect with those who are striving to make their marriage better. When this happens, you will naturally strive to improve your marriage. Likewise, connecting with those who are known to be wise will bring you up in your desire to gain wisdom.

Someone has said, "If you're the smartest person in the room, you're in the wrong room." You need to find a person or persons who are willing to help you become a better you. These are *go-to* people. These are mentors.

How do you recognize a person who is wise and would make a good mentor? There are certain observable characteristics this person has:

A. They are not prone to panic or overreact in pressurized circumstances.
B. They are not given to extremes. They don't go off on lifestyle tangents. They don't chase the latest fads, fashions, and fears.
C. They have the benefit of age and experience. As a popular insurance company claims, "We know a thing or two, because we've seen a thing or two."
D. They make decisions based on facts not feelings. Their emotions don't get in the way of their ability to reason.

Finding the above type of person who is willing to have a close relationship with you will propel you forward in your quest for wisdom.

3-Develop the Habit of Asking Questions of Those You Meet

People generally enjoy talking about themselves. Having a conversation with them naturally develops when you ask questions. But to gain the benefit of their experience you must ask questions that are deeper than the surface. Surface questions only yield surface answers. Where are you from? What do you do for a living? Where did you go to school? These are examples of surface questions and though they may *break the ice* and aid you in getting to know someone, they will do little to develop wisdom in you.

What was the path you took to get you where you are? What has been your biggest struggle? What books have you read that really helped you? What are three things that made you most successful? These are the types of questions that develop engaging conversations resulting in genuine wisdom. When you've had a conversation with someone who has imparted wisdom to you, develop the habit of writing it down and filing it away as soon as possible. Keeping a *wisdom file* will aid you in remembering the wisdom to be gained from those you have conversed with.

4-Reflect on Your Past Mistakes

Reflecting on past mistakes is not the same as dwelling on them. When you dwell on the mistakes you've made it will discourage you and hinder you from moving ahead. It is similar to running a race while carrying a weight or wearing boots.

But if you will slow down and analyze why you did what you did and what the result was you will be in a position to avoid that mistake in the future. You must develop the ability to connect similar situations from your past with your present condition which will help you avoid making the same mistake over and over.

While driving, the idea is to glance in the rear-view mirror, not stare at it. By glancing, you can see where you've been and understand what's behind you. Staring at it while driving leads to danger and possible disaster. So, re-visit your past mistakes and determine to grow from them rather than repeat them.

5-Talk to Yourself Rather Than Listen to Yourself

Because your mind doesn't know the difference between fantasy and reality, anything that you imagine is reality to your mind. That is why bad feelings follow downward thoughts and good feelings come from good thoughts. This can be used to your advantage if you will develop the habit of thinking good thoughts. You must *visualize* in order to *actualize*. When you realize that negative thoughts are coming into your head you must stop those thoughts and replace them with better ones. You will not stop thinking, but you can control what you think about.

6-Don't Trust Your Feelings, Trust What You Know

While there is a definite place in your life for emotions, you must understand that feelings come and go and can be very misleading. They can cause you to come to conclusions that are very far from the truth.

We've all jumped to wrong conclusions based on the emotions of the moment. Perhaps you've enjoyed some time with a large group of friends. You were having a great time when one of them made a sly comment. Although the party was a huge success, that one comment is the one you go to bed with. "I wonder what he/she meant by that" or "I don't think he ever really liked me" are thoughts that tend to rattle around in your head. In reality, you had a great time and were overwhelmingly liked by those who attended the party. But *feelings* can lead you down a path that will cause you to jump to the wrong conclusions.

Maybe you've made a phone call and left a message for your friend to call you back. You don't hear from them for a while, so you call them again and leave another message. Still not hearing from them, you call a third time and request a return call. When they don't call you back you come to conclusions that are not based on facts but on your feelings regarding the facts "I wonder if they're mad at me" or, "I guess we're not as close as I thought." The only truth you know at this point is that you called them, and they have not yet returned your calls. Later you learn that their phone was stolen, and they lost all their contacts as well as their messages.

Feelings are only feelings while facts are truth. So, don't rely on your feelings, rely on the reality of what you know to be true.

7-Choose Your Battles

A wise man once said, "If you throw a rock at every barking dog, you'll never get to town." In essence, he was saying, "Choose your battles." Wise people show discernment regarding conflict. They ask the big question, "What difference does it really make?" This question is asked, in order to bring clarity to situations that can easily develop into a conflict. It is possible to win an argument and lose a friend. You must consider if the issue is important enough to risk losing a relationship. A victory over an area or subject that ultimately isn't very important brings very little satisfaction. And if it happens to cost you a friendship, the reward brings regrets.

Some age-old directives are very helpful in this area:

Rule #1: Don't sweat the small stuff!

Rule #2: It's *all* small stuff. And when you can't fight flee and when you can't flee, flow!

Before entering any conflict 5 questions should be asked:
1. Is it important?
2. What difference does it make?
3. What will this engagement cost me?
4. Is this something I feel strongly about?
5. Is this person simply looking for a fight?

A man came home from a long day at work. When he entered the living room, he noticed crayon marks on the coffee table. Something inside him snapped and he erupted in anger. "I've told Tommy time and time again, not to color on the coffee table! I'm tired of his disobedience!" Then turning his anger toward his son, he shouted, "What's the matter with you? Why can't you obey? I told you not to color on the coffee table and you did it anyway! Now go to your room!" When the situation settled down, his wife introduced perspective into the situation. She said, "I'm not going to ruin a million-dollar kid over a $100 coffee table." If the husband had asked questions number one, two, and three, perhaps he would have entered that situation with a completely different mind-set and the results may have been vastly different.

You do NOT have to attend every fight you're invited to. An honest evaluation of the situation and your role in it will enable you to sidestep difficulties and save you from engaging in worthless encounters. This is what wise people do.

8-Narrow the Focus of Your Life

Wise people are not mentally, emotionally, and physically scattered. That is to say, they discover activities worth pursuing and channel all their efforts in that direction. Their view of life is a rifle approach rather than a shotgun approach. "They are a jack of all trades and a master of none" will not be said of them.

To do this you must develop the three categories that Joseph Addison has suggested to bring clarity and direction to your life. "The three grand essentials to happiness in this life are something to do, something to love, and something to hope for."

When you have something to do, you strive to become an overcomer. Seeking a degree, saving for a vacation, completing a building project, or developing a company all fit into this category. Finding someone to love and investing your life in them brings unending satisfaction and fulfillment. Seeking something to hope for moves your life forward with anticipation and optimism and gives your life a sense of purpose.

When you spend your time developing these areas you will find that you are now focused on living a wise and joyful life of productivity and success.

9-Avoid Toxic People

Toxic people are easy to identify. They seem to be constantly complaining, bragging, criticizing, and displaying anger. With toxic people, the glass isn't just half empty, it contains bad liquid to begin with. After spending enough time with a toxic person, you will feel the need to take an emotional shower. They will drain emotionally, intellectually, and physically without replenishing that which they take from you. Because you tend to become what you are surrounded by, the toxicity of these people can rub off on you and cause you to develop their tendencies.

You must develop the discipline it takes to shield yourself from them or at least limit the time you spend with them. Support and encourage those who are toxic but find a way to do this from a distance.

Kenny died suddenly and without warning. The autopsy report revealed that he was poisoned. Soon his wife was brought in and questioned regarding the death of her husband. Upon further investigation she was released because it was discovered that although he was poisoned with arsenic, his exposure to the chemical came about by his walking in bare feet on the newly constructed deck on their home. Arsenic is a chemical that was used in the preservation process of wood. The poison entered his body through the bottom of his feet.

Just like the poison entered Kenny's body through his feet, toxic people can enter your life in many ways. You must be wise enough to understand who they are, and discreet enough to avoid them.

10-Slow Down

Without question, we live in a fast-paced world. We micro-wave our food, pile information high on Instagram, get involved in get-rich-quick schemes, and are constantly searching for faster ways to travel. No wonder why we feel the need to medicate ourselves to sleep!

Planning ahead however and being involved in intentional decision making gives you the opportunity to slow down and think through everything from key decisions to conversations. Very few decisions have to be made immediately. Knowing this helps you take the time to gather the facts from people, history, and other sources.

Slowing down brings life into focus and allows you time to enjoy your experiences while you process the information you have gathered and reflect on what you have been exposed to. Wise people take time to gain a full understanding of events and avoid jumping to conclusions and making rash decisions. In short, wise people make wise decisions because they invest the time it takes to put themselves in the best position to do so. They are sought out because they see things through the eyes of one who has thought through situations and weighed the options presented. They don't race to give a response and don't feel the need to raise their voice.

To become a wise person, you must slow down long enough to allow various aspects of life to come to you. It means you must engage in conversations with others. You must seek out opportunities gain experience in various venues. You must train your senses to see and hear more than the average person does. You must absorb information from every source you can, evaluate it, and find ways you can benefit from all those you encounter. To be a wise person, *you must* slow down!

You *can* become a wise person. But it will not happen through wishful thinking. You must pursue it as a drowning person pursues the surface. Wisdom is there for the taking. But it will not be yours unless you intentionally seek it.

- 2 -
Steps to Developing a Winning Attitude

"He had such great potential!" "She had so much going for her!" "If only they had been more committed!" These are comments made about people who came up short of expectations. They failed to reach their full potential. The fact is, it is rare that anyone reaches their full potential. We all fall short in some way or another. When the smoke clears and we look back on our achievements we conclude that in some measure, we could have done better.

When we view our potential and evaluate our performance, we will see that there is a gap between what we could have done and what we actually did. The goal in any endeavor is to close the distance or *gap* between the two. That *gap* can be used as the acrostic G.A.P. GAP can stand for G-Goals, A-Attitude, P-Persistence. For our purposes we are going to focus on the center of that acrostic. We are going to look at attitude and see how that affects everything we do and learn how to shape our attitudes in order to heighten our performance.

Regardless of whether we are talking about how well we do in athletics, business, or our home life, attitude plays such a big part in how we perform. To paraphrase what Zig Ziglar has said, "It's your attitude, not your aptitude, that gives you altitude and intestinal fortitude."

The right attitude will help you push through difficult situations. It will help you *press on* when everything in you wants to give up. It will motivate others to achieve more. A proper attitude is a winsome character trait. The best part of a good attitude is that it is available and comes by choice for us all. Don't miss that! Developing a good attitude is a choice, but it is an achievable objective and starts with basic steps we must intentionally take.

1-Take Control of Your Attitude

No one, and that means "NO ONE" can *make* you feel a particular way. No one can shape your attitude but you. Your attitude, how you view things and how you respond to them, is completely under your control. You can determine if you feel good, bad, happy, successful, sad, or insignificant. Realizing this is the first step in taking control of your attitude.

For some, this is a very difficult concept to grasp. They have been pressed down by so many people and circumstances for so long, that it is a huge struggle to see a positive outcome in any situation. They believe that every day is a rainy Monday and that the light at the end of the tunnel is nothing more than an on-coming train. Although it is very difficult for them to turn their negative outlook in a positive direction it is still possible and *still* within their control.

Taking control of your attitude is every bit an intentional choice as choosing what to eat, what to wear, or what type of car to buy. When you determine that you need an *attitude adjustment* you must consciously decide that you will change your thinking. This will lead to a change in attitude, causing a change in response.

This is clearly seen in the life of a small boy at play. One day, a mother looked out her back-door window to see her young son holding a bat a ball. She could hear him yell to an invisible crowd as he threw the ball up and swung the bat. "I am the greatest batter in the world!" But each time he swung he failed to come close to hitting the ball. She felt so bad for him. But just before she opened the door to offer him some encouragement, she saw him put his hands on his hips, turn to the great crowd and announce, "I am the greatest pitcher in the world!"

2-Stop Listening to Yourself and Start Talking to Yourself

Negative thoughts can bombard your mind relentlessly. They are sponsored by those in the advertising world but also originate deep in the recesses of our minds. Part of the goal of those marketing products is to convince you that you don't have enough, know enough, are happy enough, or are good enough as you are. You need their product to make you and your life better. When you are told this over and over the tendency is to question your own feelings about yourself. This can lead to a downward spiral regarding your own self-worth.

To reverse this trend, you must replace the thoughts you have that are negative with ones that are positive in order to lift you up and keep you moving forward.

In 1944, Johnny Mercer wrote the lyrics to a song the chorus of which went, "Accentuate the positive. Eliminate the negative. Latch on to the affirmative. Don't mess with Mr. In-between." We would do well to follow that advice.

Begin by telling yourself good things about yourself. Phrases like, "I am kind! My hair looks good! I like myself! I have lots of friends!" and "This is going to be a great day!" This will go a long way toward pointing your attitude in the right direction.

Next, start dreaming good dreams. Use your imagination to think about good things. Think about the possibility of good outcomes. Ask, "What's the best thing that can happen today and what can I do to bring that about?" Someone has wisely noted, "When your memories exceed your dreams, you begin to die." Don't let yourself and your dreams, desires, and expectations die. Dream and dream big. Talk yourself into having a good attitude.

3-Get Proper Rest

Lack of proper rest truncates so many aspects of our lives. Emotions, reason, determination, perspective, and a proper attitude are all thrown off kilter when fatigue is present. Understanding the need to pull back and rest is every bit as important as the grit it takes to press on. Developing the discipline to retire early at the end of the day is as important as getting up to start your day.

What is getting in the way of a good night's sleep? Worries, anger, fear, and distractions (like television) can all block us from a good night's rest. You must evaluate these obstacles and take measures to counter their effects. Perhaps reading a good book, listening to relaxing music, or writing to a friend are the antidote you need to move you into a position to let go and drift off to sleep.

Ecclesiastes 10:10 says, "If the ax is dull and its edge unsharpened, more strength is needed, but skill will bring success." Part of that skill is simply recognizing when it is time to cut off the effort, re-group, and re-charge your energies. Re-sharpening your *ax* is paramount to the success of any endeavor. Proper rest is essential to developing a positive attitude.

4-Enter and Exit Your Time of Sleep with Positive Thoughts

Your first and last thoughts of the day are very important in shaping both how well you rest and how well you begin your day. When closing your eyes on the day it is important to focus on all the good things that occurred that day. Thinking good thoughts brings you to a point of thankfulness and peace. Being appreciative of a warm bed, a cool house, health, employment, family, and friends are all topics bringing satisfaction and contentment.

Starting your day with good thoughts will initiate emotional momentum and get you moving in the proper mental direction. This idea is captured in the following writing:

> This is the beginning of a new day. I can waste it or use it for good. What I do today is important because I am exchanging a day of my life for it. When tomorrow comes, this day will be gone forever, leaving in its place something I have traded for it. I want it to be a gain, not a loss; good, not evil; success, not failure — in order that I shall not regret the price I paid for it because the future is just a whole string of nows.

5-Be Around Positive People

You will become what you surround yourself with! If you spend your time with those who are positive and uplifting, you will find yourself gravitating toward positive thoughts and attitudes. Conversely, if you run in the circles of negative people, you will notice that your thoughts and feelings spiral in a downward direction. The attitudes of your associates will either bring you up or pull you down. There are very few neutral relationships. You must evaluate your associates and determine if they are lifting you up or pulling you down.

Positive friends lift you up. They show up when tough times come. They bring a smile to your face and encourage you. Positive friends bring laughter to your life and support you.

In the movie *As Good As It Gets*, Jack Nicholson plays the part of a neurotic, obsessive/compulsive writer who befriends (unnerves and annoys) Helen Hunt. At one point in the movie, he wins her friendship and affection when he declares, "You make me want to be a better person." That's what good friends with positive attitudes do. They make you a better you!

6-Develop the Habit of Re-Visiting Your Victories

This is not a directive to live in the past. It is a suggestion to think about (not dwell on) those things in your life that have gone well. Your mind does not know the difference between reality and fantasy. It cannot distinguish between a memory, and what is actually happening. That is why you become frightened at a scary movie and feel good just thinking about what you would do with the money you won in the lottery. When you play those scenarios in your mind it interprets it as actually taking place and gives your body the emotional bent that naturally would occur if it was real. That is one of the reasons your thought life is vital to the shaping of your attitude.

Thinking on your victories can do the same for your attitude. How did it feel? What led up to that victory? What were the good things that came out of it?

Re-visiting your victories will automatically cause you to conclude that because of past victories future success is possible. It will make you feel like a winner and when you feel like a winner you gain the confidence it takes to engage in activities that can bring about victories further enhancing your *resume* of winning.

7-Stop Re-Reading the History of Your Losses

Along with re-visiting your victories, comes the caution of camping out on your losses. While it is true that you can and should learn from your mistakes, that is quite different from concentrating on them and allowing them to shape your future. Losses may include, failure in a task or class, hurtful words from critics, the loss of a job, the dissolution of a marriage, negative encounters with others, and a host of other things.

Regarding your losses, you must understand: Your past is NOT your future. Too many people cannot start a new chapter in their lives because they are too busy reading the old chapters.

The reason why the windshield in your car is so much bigger than the rear-view mirror is because the direction you most want to head is forward, not backward. Is there a need for a rear-view mirror? Absolutely. It can be of great help to you when you need to see what's behind you. But most of your time should be spent looking through the windshield at what's up ahead, not what is behind. Likewise, a successful life is built on looking ahead, into the future, not at the past, and most importantly, not at the past mistakes and losses.

The soccer superstar, Pele once said, "Success isn't determined by how much you win, but by how you play the week after you lose." It is in planning, preparing, and looking forward to the future that you develop a winning attitude and move your life ahead.

8-Develop a *Long-View* Mentality

It's been said, "A set-back is a set-up for a come-back." This can only be embraced when you look at more than what's right in front of you. From ground level mountains are enormous and give you a particular appreciation for their size and beauty. But when you fly above the mountains, you get an entirely different perspective. Somehow, they don't seem so large and the task of climbing them doesn't seem so daunting. That's what it's like when you take the long-view of life. Trials, problems, and difficult situations can be handled better when you break them down and don't see them all at once.

Looking at past victories as well as others' examples can be great tools in developing the proper perspective. Questions such as: "What will I learn from this?" and "How will I grow from this?" may be important in developing the long-view mentality you need. Statements such as, "Other people have done this, I can too!" and "This is not the hardest thing I've ever done!" can also help you get through difficult situations and tough seasons in your life.

The idea of a *long-view* mentality is seen in the illustration of a man who was ship-wrecked on an island in the Pacific Ocean. As time went on and no rescue developed, he began building with the idea of long-term survival. He built a shelter to sleep in, a storage facility, a shed for firewood, a hammock, and several other items to make his lonely life more bearable. Each day began with a prayer for his rescue. Each night he fell asleep with the same request. After being on the island for over a month, he found himself in a lightning storm. The wind threatened to blow his hut apart, so he sought the protection of a nearby cave. While in the cave, lightning struck his home and structures burning everything to the ground.

The next morning found him sitting next to the smoldering remains of all he had built. As he sat in the sand, he became more and more angry at God. "Why? Why did you take everything that I had?" With tears streaming down his face he shook his fist heavenward and screamed, "I had so little and you took even that!" With those words he lay on his face in the sand and longed for death.

The outpouring of emotions put him to sleep. An hour later he awoke with the touch of a man's hand. He rolled over and came face to face with several men who were there to rescue him.

After boarding their ship, the man asked, "I lost all hope of being rescued. How did you find me?" One of the men replied, "We never would have found you if you hadn't sent up such a large smoke signal." It was then that the man realized the good outcome from his bad circumstances.

Developing a long view will change your attitude. It will help you look at your life and circumstances in a way that will enable you to lift your head and move forward even during very trying times.

9-View Your Obstacles as Opportunities

Life is full of obstacles. Some come at us in unexpected ways. Some are very un-welcomed. The loss of a job or loved one, health issues, and financial difficulties are examples of tough situations we would prefer to avoid. Other obstacles come to us by our own doing. They are challenges we seek to overcome in order to develop character traits in us and build a good story. Athletic competition, educational pursuits, and health related issues are obstacles we put in place to bring us to the next level in our lives.

No matter how the difficulty comes, overcoming it will build you into a stronger person on some level. It could increase your emotional, physical, spiritual, mental strength, or a combination of any of these.

Overcoming difficulties is euphoric. It brings a satisfaction like no other pursuit. That's why so many people engage in physical challenges. When the goal is reached, the satisfaction of reaching it does something deep within the soul of the person.

Some of the other benefits of overcoming challenges include:
- It empowers others. Intrinsically, people understand, *what one person can do, others can do*. This helps them continue amidst their challenge. It inspires others and gives them the courage not to quit. Your victory stands as an example for them to follow.
- It builds confidence in you for bigger things. Once you over-

come something, you have the confidence to meet other challenges. Your mentality becomes, *Because I did that, I can do this!*
- It develops *categorical assurance*. When you feel like a winner in a particular area (physically, educationally, financially), you approach other areas like a champion and feel less intimidated.

Our natural tendency is to avoid struggle and pain-to become comfortable in our hearts and minds. But as any champion will tell you, comfortable people rarely do anything worthy of honor and emulation. There are no statues dedicated to mediocrity! When your *want-to* becomes your *have-to*, then your *possibly* becomes your *probably*!

There is a distinct difference between a buffalo and a cow. Buffaloes are independent. Cows however, in many ways, are dependent. Another difference between the buffalo and the cow is found in how they handle storms. When a storm comes, cows panic and run from the wind, rain, and thunder. Buffaloes on the other hand, react quite differently when faced with wind, rain, and thunder. They run into the storm thereby coming out the other side much sooner. Cows run from the storm, are caught by the storm, and spend more time in the storm.

When obstacles come into your life, don't ignore and avoid them. Lean into them. Run toward them. Face them head on. You will find that you will grow stronger from your experience with them and you will get through them much quicker.

10-Become Generous

Generosity is a winsome character trait. So many people and organizations benefit from those who have a giving mentality. But generosity also has a peripheral effect. It carries with it great benefits for those who exercise it.

Some of the best qualities of generosity include:
- It is a choice. It is totally within your power to choose to be generous or not.
- It is not regulated to the giving of money. Time, wisdom, talent, kindness, and empathy are all commodities. You don't have to have money to be generous. You just have to have the mindset to be generous.
- Because generosity goes beyond the bounds of money, everyone has something worth giving and the power to give it.

Martin of Tours was a man in whom faith and works combined to make him a true Christian. One day he met a beggar who asked for alms. Martin didn't have any money, but he saw that the beggar was freezing, so he gave him what he had. He took off his soldier's overcoat, old and faded as it was, cut it in half, and wrapped half around the beggar. During the night Martin had a dream. He saw heaven opened, and Christ wearing half an overcoat. One of the angels asked, "Lord, why are you wearing that shabby old coat?" Christ answered, "Because my servant gave it to me."

Becoming generous gives you the understanding that you are making a difference in someone's life and this brings meaning to your own life. It brings you great satisfaction in knowing that the world is a better place because you are in it.

Generosity brightens your day, fills your heart with satisfaction, impacts others, and generally goes a great way toward giving you a positive attitude about life.

A winning attitude is readily seen in this writing by J.L. Borges:

> *If I could live my life again*
> *I'd try to make more mistakes.*
> *I wouldn't try to be so perfect.*
> *I'd be more relaxed.*
> *I'd be more true-to-life than I was.*
> *In fact, I'd take fewer things seriously.*
> *I'd be less hygienic.*
> *I'd take more risks.*
> *I'd take more trips.*
> *I'd watch more sunsets.*
> *I'd climb more mountains.*
> *I'd swim more rivers.*
> *I'd go to more places I've never been.*
> *I'd eat more ice cream and less lima beans.*
> *I'd have more real problems and less imaginary ones.*
> *I was one of those people who live prudent and prolific lives each minute of their existence.*
> *Of course, I did have moments of joy. Yet if I could go back, I'd try to have good moments only.*
> *In case you don't know, that's what life is made of.*
> *I was one of those who never go anywhere,*

Intentional Steps: The Pathway to Better Living

without a thermometer,
without a hot-water bottle,
without an umbrella,
without a parachute.
If I could live again
I'd travel light,
I'd try to walk barefoot,
from Spring to Fall.
I'd ride more merry-go-rounds.
I'd watch more sunrises,
play with more kids.

- 3 -
Steps to a Richer Marriage

Marriage is the most concentrated form or human relationships. It has the potential to drive a couple together in an unbreakable iron-like bond, or expose each other to faults, personalities, and attitudes that drive them apart. Those who claim that marriage is an easy road have either never been married or have not been paying attention. To be successfully married takes a commitment on both parties to work.

But the emphasis needs to be placed less on *staying* married (avoiding divorce) and more on being *successfully* married. This is where it becomes most difficult. Measuring marital success is part of the challenge. How do you know you are achieving success in your marriage? Two questions must be asked that will indicate success. Both of these questions must be asked of each member and both must be answered in the affirmative. Along with this, the questions should not be asked until sufficient time has passed since the wedding. These questions are for the more *seasoned* couples.

Question 1: If your life was to be as it is now, and you could go back in time, would you marry the same person again?

Question 2: Is your marriage the type of marriage you want your children to have?

If each of you can honestly answer *yes* to both of these questions, then it is very likely you have a successful marriage.

Now let's look at some of the key ingredients it takes to gain and maintain a successful marital union.

1-Discover Your Mate's Love Language and Commit to Speak It to Them Regularly and Sacrificially

According to Dr. David Chapman, love is expressed to others primarily in one of five ways: gifts, acts of service, quality time, touch, and words of affirmation. When affection is expressed through one of these five ways the receiver understands the message of love. Most people, however, assume that their love language is everyone else's love language and they speak only that and thereby run the risk of not communicating love in the highest sense. It is very important that you study your mate to discover what needs to be done to send a clear and consistent *love message* their way.

Beyond this, you must be willing to speak it in creative ways. A person's love language may be gifts but, sending them flowers three times a week may soon lose its luster. You need to think it through and find different ways of speaking the same language of love.

Coupled with creativity is the idea of sacrifice. When your mate understands that the love language is spoken through the teeth of sacrifice the *volume* is turned up. Giving up time with friends to spend it with your spouse is an example of speaking sacrificial language. If a woman takes a day off of work and spends part of her time washing her husband's car, he will hear *I love you* loud and clear. The key is to target your partner's love language in such a way that it demonstrates forethought (creativity) and sacrifice. When all this is combined the only conclusion your husband and wife can come to is that they are deeply loved and cared for.

2-Continue to Date

Too often, the marriage relationship is taken for granted. A couple will *settle in* and get so comfortable that the relationship is put on auto-pilot and life is best characterized as routine. This is when boredom and dry seasons settle in. You must fight this by continuing to pursue the affections of your mate. This is best done by intentionally dating one another.

Some couples have a *date night* each week. Because of schedules, not everyone can establish this, so dates have to be planned out in a different way. The first step is to define what a date is. A date doesn't have to be dinner and a movie. A date doesn't have to be expensive. It doesn't have to be long or encompass the entire evening. It doesn't even have to happen in the evening.

A date can be (but is not limited to), a long walk in the country, working on a hobby together, watching a sunset, cooking a special meal together, reading together, gardening, attending an outdoor concert, or any number of other activities. Being together, enjoying one another's company, and discovering more and more about each other are the key ingredients to successful dating.

3-Dream and Share Goals

Someone has rightly observed that when our memories exceed our dreams, we begin to die. This is no less true in the marital relationship. Revisiting the past is a healthy exercise. Attempting to re-live the past will make it difficult to move forward as a couple.

Financial goals, vacation desires, retirement planning, recreational aspirations are examples of some of the categories couples can spend time discussing, dreaming about, and developing a plan for achieving what they want.

Questions such as: In five years, where do you see us? If money were not an object, what would you do? If you could travel anywhere in the world, where would you like to go? If we owned our own island, who would we invite to live with us there? These are examples of dream topics and can be used to launch us into some lively discussion.

Questions such as: What do we need to do to get a bigger house? How can we save for a vacation in Europe? Is there a way we can make owning our own business a reality? Questions like these can bring us to the point of setting goals and making them a reality.

It is vitally important that we guard against letting our marriages grow stale, cold, and routine. This is off-set by intentionally dreaming and planning to make our dreams come true.

4-Commit to Clear Communication

Communication difficulties can plague any marriage. Distractions, time constraints, emotions, and lack of effort get in the way of the ability to share thoughts, ideas, and desires. But certain tools can be used to establish and foster better communication.

A word picture that may be helpful is to see the act of communicating as a tennis match. One person has the ball at a particular time. They lob the ball into the other person's court and that person is given the opportunity to lob it back. When the ball is not hit back, communication efforts are interrupted. Some helpful guidelines are called for if we are going to have a successful volley.

1. You must commit to listening with the idea of understanding. Larry King once said, "I never learned anything while talking."
2. Practice *Listener's Lean*. This is the posture in which you listen. Leaning forward tells the other person, "I'm here and I'm interested"
3. Listen with your face. Along with body posture is facial engagement. Looking the person in the eye tells them "You have all my attention."
4. Eliminate distractions. Phones, computers, music, texts, and people can get in the way of conversation. You may have to find both a designated time as well as a secluded place to discuss items of importance.
5. Position yourselves for ease of communication. Men and women tend to communicate with different postures. Generally, women feel comfortable in a face-to-face position while men feel more at ease side-by side. So how do you determine which posture works best? The answer is, the posture to be assumed should be determined by the person who is in need of the discussion. If the woman wants to talk about something that is bothering her, sitting across from one another would be preferred. If the man wants to talk about their schedules, then perhaps sitting on the couch or going for a ride is desirable.

If a couple will intentionally commit to developing clear communication skills, so many of their problems will be side-stepped or eliminated. They will have a clearer sense of the heart of their mate which will help solidify their relationship and make room for years of fulfillment.

5-Fight Cleanly

There is a distinct difference between successful couples and unsuccessful couples. The difference surfaces very clearly with how they disagree. When conflicts arise in the case of bad couples, each press for a victory. Good couples, however, press for a resolution. They agree to disagree agreeably.

Some key points need to be made that will help couples resolve

conflict when disagreements occur.
- A. Stick to the subject. Avoid bringing up every detail and introducing topics that have nothing to do with the disagreement. Introducing peripheral issues is called a *kitchen sink* argument and will do nothing in bringing resolution.
- B. Avoid name calling. There is no place in the marriage relationship for addressing each other in a derogatory manner.
- C. If forgiveness has been granted, do not bring up the past. When you harken back to a former event that has been forgiven, you demonstrate that you have not in fact, granted forgiveness.
- D. Understand that emotions are valid. Though they may not be accurate, a person's feelings must be recognized and given respect. Brushing aside a person's feelings of hurt, fear, or embarrassment reveals an uncaring attitude.

When we accept the fact that disagreements are inevitable in every long-term relationship, we can better prepare ourselves to deal with them. We can be equipped to meet conflict head on and disarm the problem before it grows into something more difficult to handle.

6-Develop Close Relationships with Other Couples Who Are Experiencing Successful Marriages

Spending time with other couples who demonstrate success in marriage can be a great benefit. They can be called a *home team*. Much like a sports team, your *home team* will be there for you with advice, support, encouragement and an example worth following.

Generally, but not necessarily, this couple will be older with some years of experience under their belt. They have weathered various storms and have learned how to navigate rough waters. They are available and ready to help you when you need it. You will find that you enjoy being around them and that your time with them always adds to your relationship with each other.

Being around others who are doing well in their marriage will add wisdom, encouragement, resources, and a successful example to follow for your marriage.

7-Make Your Spouse Your Priority

This directive becomes controversial when children are involved. Many feel as long as children are in the home, they take precedence over everything else including the husband and wife. The question naturally comes up, *then what?* When the children are the center of attention in the family two things happen. They develop a sense of entitlement. They conclude that the family exists to make them happy. Along with that you are left with the remnants of a relationship where your spouse is given *emotional and relational leftovers*. When the children leave home, each of you finds yourself staring at a person you no longer really know. Deep inside each of you understands that they are not held in high esteem.

However, when the children see that mom and dad love each other deeply and are completely committed to their marriage they develop a sense of security regarding the family and their place in it.

Your spouse needs to have complete confidence that they are a priority to you. They take first place above work, friends, recreation, and even children.

8-Protect Your Spouse

One of the ways to demonstrate that your spouse is your priority is by protecting them. Generally, you'll find that men are physically stronger than women. This enables them to protect their wives from physical harm. This is seen by walking on the *danger* side of the road- the side where traffic is and the side where aggressive dogs live. This also means that when the doorbell rings he should get up to answer it.

Men, on the other hand need internal protection. Men tend to be much more emotionally sensitive than they want others to know. Their egos need protection. A wife can provide that protection in ways that no one else can. Support and encouragement are her two greatest tools.

Furthermore, husbands and wives can protect each other from *toxic* people. The truth is, in all of our lives there are those in our social circles who drain us mentally and emotionally. This can also take its toll on us physically. Recognizing who these *friends* are is the first step in protecting your spouse from over-exposure to those who are toxic. Protecting your mate's schedule, running *interference* for them, and advising them to limit their time with these people will go a long way toward protecting them from becoming *infected*.

9-Be Patient

Being with someone, anyone, requires a certain amount of patience.

Sometimes people rub you the wrong way and you have to intentionally remove yourself from their presence. But when you are in a marital relationship, there is no *escape*. There are times when your commitment to marriage may seem more like a life sentence. You thought you were marrying a dreamboat, but often they seem more like a ship-wreck.

Keep in mind that when you marry, you are essentially marrying three people. You marry who they are. You marry who you think they are. And finally, you marry who they become because they are married to you. So, in essence, if you are not happy with who they are, you are in fact, partly to blame.

It is not possible to have a perfect *machine* when the parts are damaged. Likewise, having the perfect marriage is not possible because the two main parts are damaged. With this in mind, it behooves us to deal with our spouse with a large measure of patience.

Rule number one: Don't sweat the small stuff. Rule number two: It's all small stuff! And if you can't fight flee, and if you can't flee flow!

10-Work to Make Your Marriage Better

You will never have the perfect marriage. It started going downhill when you were announced as husband and wife. Although it will never be perfect, it can always get better. There is a next level to marriage that is attainable. But you must commit to investing in the available tools for improvement.

Too often we view marriage in the same way a fisherman views the act of fishing. When a fish is in the boat, he no longer thinks about the bait. He has what he has pursued, and he has won *the prize*. In marriage, we tend to neglect the *bait* because we have won *the prize*. We take for granted our mates and stop pursuing them and doing the things that attracted them to us in the first place.

The truth of the matter is, that which got you to where you are rarely keeps you at that level. You must continually pursue your spouse. It takes much time and effort, but you must always look for ways to reinvent yourself as the seasons of marriage come and go.

Books, seminars, studies, retreats, and the counsel of others are in plentiful supply. Availing yourself of them is the key. That is where effort on your part comes in.

If you will do what it takes to keep your marriage fresh and healthy, both you and your lifetime mate will come to the conclusion that you've achieve *the catch of a lifetime*!

Although having a successful marriage takes great energy, patience, and training, if the effort is made to make it work, the rewards will be well worth it. You will develop a relationship with someone that is fulfilling, exciting, and deeply satisfying. You will find yourself married to a person whom you look forward to growing old with, and you will have a union that is worth repeating and a marriage you would be happy to have your children duplicate.

- 4 -
Steps to Academic Growth

Some people are born with certain abilities that make it easier for them to find success in the academic world. They think differently, have great concentration skills, and are driven to succeed on-line or in the classroom. Others have to work hard to find the same level of success. They are easily distracted, bored, have a poor learning environment and struggle to stay motivated. Wherever you are on the learning spectrum, whether on-line or in the traditional classroom setting, there are some key habits that can be developed that will help you reach the next level in your academic pursuits.

1-Attend Class and Be on Time

No contact-no impact. When you attend class, it develops a rapport with your instructor. It allows you to ask questions and clarify material. Being with other students in the classroom also builds momentum and motivation to learn. Being on time shows respect to your instructor and builds eagerness and openness. Plan ahead. Leave early enough to arrive on time. Make your plans the night before so your schedule allows you to arrive when expected.

2-Take Good Notes

The joke is told about a college professor who was lecturing the first day of class. The students were furiously taking notes. He stopped mid-sentence and said, "Listen, you don't have to write down everything I say verbatim." A student raised his hand and asked, "How do you spell verbatim?"

A dull pencil remembers more than a sharp mind! Whether from a lecture or from a book, learn to take *statement notes*. Statement notes capture the main thought that is spoken or written. If something is repeated verbally, it is important. Summarize it and write it down. In a book, the key points are generally found in the opening sentence of a paragraph with the rest of the paragraph used to clarify or emphasize the opening point. You cannot keep up by reading everything assigned so learn to summarize in your notes. Before the next class read over your textbook and lecture notes. This will put you in line with what you are about to hear in class or on-line.

3-In the Classroom, Sit Up Front
Sitting up front is beneficial for several reasons:
- It puts you in a place of accountability. You can't sleep, use your phone or stare out the window, day dreaming when. You know there are authoritative eyes upon you.
- It demonstrates respect for the instructor. This will build rapport between you and your teacher.
- It forces you to pay attention.
- It limits distractions. Because you're up close to the front, distracting activities are more likely to be behind you and out of view.

4-Develop a Study Style That Fits Your Learning Style
Just as people have different personalities, people have individual styles for learning. Some have to have complete silence while others can handle background noise. Some sit still and pour over books and notes while others do better when they move about. Discover your learning style and build a study environment that meets that learning style.

If you are able to listen to music when studying, make sure it is low so as not to be a distraction. If you lean more toward auditory learning, read your notes out loud, even to the point of presenting them to yourself. If you are more of a visual learner, draw pictures in your mind of the scene from the book. Some learning calls for rote memorization (math equations or chemistry formulas). Memorize them by using an association or repetition method.

Develop a *study island*. This is a place you go to exclusively to study. It is isolated from distractions and allows you to verbalize the lesson without interfering with others. On your *island* you are isolated and do nothing but study. If the phone rings, you must get up and walk away in order to have a conversation. Limit visits from friends and develop the discipline needed to do nothing but study on your *island*.

5-When Possible, Find a Study Partner

None of us is as smart as all of us. With this in mind, it behooves you to go beyond studying on your *study island* and to meet with a study partner or study team. The singular purpose for meeting is for better understanding of the material. This should be with those who are good students motivated to learn. This *meeting* should be only about the subject and should not carry any social activity to it. It needs to be on the level of a business meeting in a company.

6-Ask Clarifying Questions

Whether on line or in the classroom, do not be afraid to ask clarifying questions. For some this is very difficult because speaking in the presence of others is intimidating. Sitting up front may be a big help in overcoming this fear. When asking these questions reword the statement in your mind and then verbalize it. For example, when the instructor says, "It's been said that Washington's biggest asset was not his army, but his spies." You may ask, "So are you saying that without the use of those spies, the outcome of the revolutionary war was in jeopardy?" Or you may ask a clarifying question. When it is stated, "In 2005, Hurricane Katrina hit the area of New Orleans devastating the city." You may ask, "How many lives were lost?" or What was the financial loss?"

By re-wording statements or asking clarifying questions, you personalize the material and take ownership of it. Hearing your own voice and thinking through the material internalizes it and makes it easier to recall.

7-Get Proper Sleep

The amount of sleep a person needs varies among individuals. But lack of sufficient rest interferes with reason, emotions, and the ability to focus. It takes an equal amount of discipline to go to bed at a reasonable hour as it does to get up and go to class. Proper rest is imperative to learning. The adage "A dull ax makes you exert more force" is very true.

Sleep is part of the learning triangle. There are three sides to a student's academic life: Social, educational, and rest. You must pick two of the three to be emphasized above the third. If you want an active social life and solid academics, sleep will suffer. If you want a great academic experience and a healthy amount of sleep, your social life will be truncated. If you want a busy social life but lots of sleep, it will show up in your GPA. A wise student will choose academics and proper sleep.

8-Treat Your Educational Experience as If It Was a Job
Most full-time students are not full-time employees at the same time. But if you treat your classroom time as if it was work time, you will gain the full benefit of the educational experience. Showing up for class prepared, dressed properly, and on time with the proper attitude will go a long way toward making you a success academically. Be as committed to your educational time as you would to an employment scenario, and you'll find that success will come your way.

Your payment for doing a good job academically? Knowledge, confidence, experience, and positioning for success in the job market.

9-Eat Well
Just as the proper amount of sleep is necessary for good brain functioning, so is a solid diet. Food is your energy source both for the body and the brain. Try to avoid foods that make you sleepy or interfere with good digestion. The key is to eat a wide variety of foods that agree with you in moderation. Your car cannot run well without the proper fuel, and neither can your brain.

10-Engage in Your Assignments Early
Usually, a course will require a project, paper, or presentation with a set deadline. These requirements most often will be assigned and explained at the beginning of the semester. Attack the assignment as early in the semester as you can with the understanding that you will have requirements from the other classes you are taking.

Engaging in your assignments early has several clear advantages:
- It lightens your load later in the semester.
- It establishes a good work habit.
- It keeps you out of panic mode.
- It gives you time to review it and make corrections or adjust-

ments.
- It ensures quality.
- It gives a feeling of accomplishment.
- It builds academic momentum.

As is the case for all areas of responsibility, doing it right is better than doing it over.

- 5 -
Steps to Experiencing Financial Success

Money is important. It provides opportunity, eases struggle, and offers some level of security. Someone has jokingly said, "Money isn't everything, but it sure makes poverty easier to live with." The truth is, money can be of great benefit to any individual or group. But acquiring money can also be a point of contention and can bring disastrous results. The top three topics married couples struggle with are communication, money, and in-laws with money being at the top of the list. The list of those who have been *given* large sums of money leading to a horrific end is long and growing. There is a clear difference between having possessions and your possessions having you. The key is balance-keeping money and your attitude toward wealth in proper perspective. Following are principles (not guarantees) that will help you see money in the right light thereby side-stepping difficulties others have experienced while pursuing financial gains.

1-Accept the Fact That You Can Spend a Dollar Any Way You Want, But You Can Only Spend It Once

When you realize that your resources are limited, you pay closer attention to the handling of them. With this idea in mind you begin to discern the difference between a *want* and a *need*. We often confuse these words and don't understand that there is a distinct difference between the two. But when we slow down and really evaluate our words, we understand that a *want* is not the same as a *need*. "I need a new car" is followed by the reason "I want a new car." If the current car is dependable and does what we ask of it, then the word *need* will be accurately changed to *want*. With this in mind, four helpful questions

should be asked:
1. Is it really a need?
2. If I really do need it, do I need it now?
3. Is what I'm purchasing worth the money I'm spending for it?
4. Will it last?

Responsible spending will follow closely on the heels of these four questions.

2-Save Some, Spend Some, Give Some Away

This discipline will bring financial balance into your life. Saving some will birth fiscal responsibilities. Spending some will usher in enjoyment and experiences. Giving some away (preferably anonymously) will help those around you and is followed by personal joy and satisfaction.

3-Diversify Your Streams of Income

Beyond the salary you are paid by your employer, it is wise to have other means by which your bank account can grow. This money can be set aside to do the extra things (like vacations, or meeting others' needs) that you desire to do. A hobby that you enjoy, can be a good way to pad your income. Repurposing items, tutoring, detailing vehicles, handyman work, book writing, recycling metal, garage sales, pet sitting, and catering are just a few examples of spare-time activities that can be added to your income.

When you do this, extra resources are at your disposal when layoffs come, or personal economic down-turns occur and will help steady your *financial ship*. The key here is to carve out some free time to bring added income.

4-Develop Marketable Job Skills

Developing job skills will help you diversify your streams of income. This can be done formally, by taking particular classes, or informally by teaching yourself. It may be in an area in which you are already working such as a nurses' aid attending nursing classes, or in a niche that you have an interest in like a teacher who enjoys art or woodworking.

5-Invest Early and Consistently

Finding solid investments is the key to building wealth. Simple mathematics demonstrates that when you invest early you put yourself in a position to have your money work for you. Just $1,000 a year ($83 per month) at 5% will yield over $13,200 in ten years. In twenty years that same ten-year investment (with no further additions) will yield $21,500. If the fiscal habit of investing $1,000 each year was continued for the full twenty years, that $20,000 would yield over $34,700.

In the stock market, consistent investing is called *dollar averaging*. In this scenario of investing, a set amount of money is invested in a particular stock regardless of the fluctuations in the market. When the stock rises less shares are purchased, but their value is higher. When the stock dips, more shares are bought maintaining the value of the portfolio.

6-Resist Acquiring Debt

It's been said, "When your out-go exceeds your income, then your upkeep will become your down fall." You would be hard pressed to find anyone willing to look at an item and then decide they want to pay more for it. But making purchases with a credit card without the ability to pay it back immediately, is in fact, an agreement to a price increase for that item.

According to the Federal Reserve, credit card debt surpassed the $1 trillion mark in 2017. The average American carries over $6,000 in credit card debt alone. When you owe $6,000 at an average interest rate of 16% you will pay an extra $960 each year for an item that you may or may not currently have. So, you must ask yourself, "What could I do with an extra $960?" This type of thinking may change your mind about acquiring debt so easily.

The key to resisting credit card debt is to pay in cash whenever possible. When you pay in cash, the tendency is to spend less. This is due to the fact that visually you are seeing yourself parting with your money. Because there tends to be an emotional attachment to our money, it hurts to part with it.

A very popular slogan from a prominent credit company is, "What's in your wallet?" Fiscal responsibility would allow you to answer, "My cash!"

7-Find a Trusted Investment Advisor

For most of us investing can be extremely complicated. We need advice, which is in abundance, from those who are wise and can point us in the right direction which tends to be a rarity. When looking for someone to help you in making investment decisions, it is imperative that you enlist the help of someone who has spent sufficient time in the industry coupled with a successful track record.

These counselors talk about tendencies, not guarantees. They will speak of diversification rather than putting all your eggs in one basket. They will look at the big picture over the long haul instead of the *latest (and greatest) deal*. They will evaluate your risk factor rather than use a blanket *one-size-fits-all* approach.

8-Exercise Deferred Gratification

This is an area many are not comfortable with. As Americans, we want what we want, when we want it, and how we want it. But emotional purchases rarely satisfy. We have a tendency to buy things we don't need, with money we don't have, to impress people we don't like. Deferred gratification puts us in a position to by-pass emotions when purchasing items.

Deals come and go and eventually come back again. Resisting an emotional attachment to an item can go a long way toward giving you the will power to say *No* or *Not yet* to a particular purchase which later may lead to regret.

Getting the advice of a friend, looking at the big picture, or waiting twenty-four hours before making a big purchase will aid you in exercising deferred gratification.

9-Develop a Reasonable Budget

Living within your means is the best way to finding financial peace and freedom. The quickest way to do that is to develop a sound budget.

Some of the benefits to having a budget include:
- It reveals hidden expenses.
- It allows for emergencies.
- It helps you save for future needs and wants.
- It brings an awareness of how much you have.
- It contributes to debt-free living.
- It puts you and your spouse on the same financial page.
- It frees you from worry.
- It gives you a sense of accomplishment.

10-Avoid Get-Rich-Quick Schemes

From those who call you on the phone, to those who advertise through the media, opportunities to *make it big* are endless. Examples of those who took advantage of these opportunities and became rich seem almost as replete. And when your imagination moves in that direction, your emotions may move you to jump in and take your chance.

But the chances of your wishes becoming a reality are as remote as Wile E. Coyote catching the Roadrunner. The best odds of winning the jackpot is in playing EuroMillions. This is presented in a total of nine countries; (Austria, Belgium, France, Ireland, Luxembourg, Portugal, Spain,

Switzerland, and the United Kingdom) Those odds of winning are 1:139,838,160. For illustrative purposes, the odds of being struck by lightning are 1:700,000.

Still, the participation in these *opportunities* persists and the temptation to join in is strong. This is evidenced by the billions that are lost each year through participation in various lotteries as well as those who join the endless number of money-making scams.

A strongly worded piece of advice: Work hard, be smart, be disciplined and invest well and the temptation to get involved in get-rich-quick schemes will diminish.

- 6 -
Steps to Effective Parenting

Those of us who have children understand Elizabeth Stone's quote, "The decision to have a child is monumental. It is to decide to forever live with your heart walking outside your body." When you take time to watch that little boy or girl while they sleep or play, the idea of your heart existing outside of your body speaks loudly and clearly. Furthermore, when you consider their life and growth and their relationship with you, you understand the adage, "Your children are a message that you will send to a world you will never meet."

Because these two ideas are true, it is vitally important to invest in these young lives and develop them into the adults both you and they need to be. What you do in your home and in the heart of that two-legged treasure will shape the adults they become. Following are ten precepts that will help you build a home environment that will foster a healthy relationship with your son or daughter.

1-Present a United Front

Although they may not understand this principle, children know the military battle plan, "Divide and conquer." This is why they will ask mom if dad says *No* and vice versa.

The antidote to this is to be united with your spouse in your child rearing philosophy. This requires lots of open discussion about all areas regarding your child. You must agree on how you will handle different situations and it is imperative that you do it before your little one arrives.

What will you do regarding the following:
- Discipline: To spank or not to spank? What does *time-out* look

like? Who is going to take the lead? Is raising one's voice permitted in your home? What behavior will we overlook and what will we address?
- Entertainment: What forms of entertainment will we allow? Will they have a T.V. in their room? What shows will we let them watch? What type of music will we allow them to listen to?
- Manners: How will they address you and each other? How will they act in public? What is acceptable behavior during meals? How do they greet strangers?
- What is the proper time for bed as it relates to their age? What does bed-time look like? Who will take the lead in preparing them for bed?

These and many more areas need to be addressed in order to develop a home of peace, order, and security. These issues must be addressed in order to provide a united front.

2-Make Your Role as a Parent a Priority

Whatever age your child is, they will only be that age for one year. In time, their independence will grow and so will yours. There will be time for golf, tennis, shopping, bridge, and whatever else you enjoy at a later date. For now, your children must take the top spot on your priority list. Parenting is a privilege (not everyone gets to be one) and your children are a gift (not everyone gets to have one). You must invest your time and energy in them while you still have the time and energy to do so. If you are there for them in their struggles, they will invite you to attend their victories.

3-Establish a Home Philosophy

One of the most difficult parts of any job is not understanding clear expectations. It is no different in your home. When your children know what is expected of them, they get a clear picture of how to behave and this leads to a strong sense of security. A home philosophy will bring this into focus. It communicates a family's core values regarding areas such as:
- Education
- Religion
- Work

- Honesty
- Relationships
- Money

A home philosophy must have four basic components:
1. It must be simple and easy to understand.
2. It must reflect the basic ideas and principles that your family values.
3. It must be reflected in the lifestyle of a mom and dad.
4. It must be posted in a place where it can be seen and referred to regularly.

Allow me to share our home philosophy. It is simply, easy to understand, and for almost two decades was displayed on the door of our refrigerator:
- God and God's word rule here.
- People matter more than things.
- Winning is measured by: Doing your best. Playing by the rules. Not quitting.

4-Love Your Spouse Supremly

Theodore Hesburgh said, "The most important thing a father can do for his children is to love their mother." This is very true and will help both your children as well as your marriage in years to come. From a marital standpoint, we must understand that through no overt fault of their own, children enter into our lives, bringing joy and frustration, drain us of great amounts of resources, and then leave. In the wake of their departure, spouses are left with a marriage that has developed over all that time. How you treat each other will have a lot to do with what you are left with in your marriage.

It also has a lot to do with how your children enter their own world after leaving your home. A home where the children are the center of attention and *rule the roost* develops insecure children who have a sense of entitlement. A home where children see a mom and dad who love each other deeply and love and care for the children as well sends out children who are secure and generous and eager to make a contribution to society.

Two key points will help build the right emotional environment for your home: https:
1. Do not be shy about displays of affection in the presence of

your children. Holding hands, hugging, kissing and embracing may be joined in by the children as they desire to share in the communication of affection.
2. Schedule dates explaining to the children that you need *daddy and mommy time*. This will send the message that they are not the center of the universe and that your love for each other is a priority.

In time, your children will realize and appreciate that they grew up in a home where dad and mom loved each other, and they will develop a desire to have the same type of relationship of their own.

5-Discipline Don't Punish

Children must understand that decisions, good or bad, bring consequences. But there is a distinct difference between punishing your child and disciplining your them. Generally, punishment is done to help you. It allows you to vent your anger and frustration with the child as the recipient. Screaming, hitting, foul language, and throwing things are all examples of punishment.

Discipline, however, is a controlled thought-out means of instructing your child and ushering them into better behavior. It is not reactionary but responsive. Remember, you are the parent. You are in charge. The ability to remain calm solidifies your position of authority.

In order to exercise discipline, there are a few things that need to be remembered:

1. Don't let the unacceptable behavior continue to the point where you lose control. If you are watching T.V. and the children are fighting in the kitchen, address it right away. Don't let it go on until you fly off the couch and head their way in a rage.
2. Periodically, change up the consequences of bad behavior. Sometimes it requires a pop on the bottom. Sometimes it calls for time-out. The loss of a privilege may be used at a different time.
3. Let the discipline fit the violation. Do not go overboard. Sometimes a parent is called to over-see behavior, and other times to over-look behavior. There is always room to extend grace.
4. Explain to your child why you are disciplining them. This can be done either before or after you have addressed the misbehavior.
5. Avoiding using your spouse as a threat. ("Wait 'til your father/mother gets home").

6-Build Memories, Not Monuments

Listen to the comments made at a funeral as the deceased is being remembered. Invariably the focus will be on time spent together and experiences shared with the departed. When people reflect on their childhood days so much more will be said about what was done rather than what was owned. Houses and offices come and go. Toys break and cars rust, but memories last forever.

Some evaluative questions will help you understand how you are doing regarding the building of memories in your home:
- Do your children talk about the time you've spent together?
- Do they enjoy coming home from school?
- Do they prefer bringing friends to your home rather than going somewhere else?
- If you gave them a choice between time going somewhere as a family or some type of toy, which would they choose?

Give your best effort to making family life full of memories to be cherished in the years to come. You will never regret it!

7-Gently Enter into Their World

It's been said, "When raising children, keep your wits about you and sit on the floor." If you will be willing to enter their world when they're young, you will be invited into their world when they are old. This is best done by exposing them to lots of experiences and activities and then paying attention to what they gravitate toward. It must be about THEM! Don't try to force them into your world. If they love tractors, take them to the sales yard and let them sit on the machines. If they love animals, trips to the zoo or books and movies about animals are in order.

8-Expect First-Time Obedience

Too often parents will give a directive and find their child totally ignoring them. Many times, this is followed by the adult beginning to count. Unless this is a math lesson, there is no reason to count. The child has come to know that obedience can be avoided until the parent gets to a certain number. It is only when that number is reached that the child responds. The problem with this scenario is that it conditions the child for delayed obedience which at some point could cause great harm. Today it's, "Come in for dinner." Tomorrow it's, "Don't run toward the road." Today it ends with them reluctantly sauntering in for a meal. Tomorrow it ends with the parents reluctantly attending their child's funeral.

If they put off obeying your authority in the home, they will learn to put off other authorities in life-teachers, police, employers. Expect first-time obedience and apply discipline when it is not observed.

9-Discover and Speak Their Love Language

According to Dr. Gary Chapman, people have a distinct language by which they interpret love: acts of service, gifts, quality time, words of affirmation, and touch. This applies to children as well as adults. Your child's love language can be discovered by looking at what they draw, listening to them speak to you and others, asking them questions and watching their actions.

Children, as well as adults will speak to you in their own love language. If you pay attention, you will discover how they interpret love. For example, a child who is constantly on your lap, hugging you, or sitting next to you may have the love language of touch. One who is always saying "I love you" or "You're a good mommy or daddy" may be speaking words of affirmation. When a loved one makes lots of things for you, he may be expressing his love by gifts. If a child always wants to help around the house or talks about being with you, they may be communicating their love language as acts of service or quality time.

When you discover what you believe is their love language, turn it back on them on a regular basis and you will be letting them know that you love and appreciate them.

10-Be the Parent, Not the Buddy

Your children will develop friendships among their peers their entire lives. You, and you alone are the only one who will fill the role as parent. Though you may feel that this will draw the two of you closer together, their need is not for another friend. Their need is for a parent. So be the parent.

This means that sometimes your response is, "Because I said so!" or "Because I'm your mother/father" or "You will not do that!" As strange as it may seem, having this relationship will create a stable environment in which your child can grow.

As time goes by you will find your role changing. Eventually they will reach full adulthood and you will become good friends. But for now, be the parent that they need, even if they don't know they need it.

When you take your role as a parent seriously and do the best you can do you will be satisfied with the outcome. Not only do you have the best chance of having a child who responds positively to your efforts, but you will be sending out a young adult who will make a positive contribution to our society.

- 7 -
Steps to Athletic Success

Whatever your level if involvement in athletics, it is important to realize that there is always room for improvement. Even the most seasoned athletes continue to reach for the next level while keeping their eyes on the basics.

Involvement in sports carries with it great benefits that go beyond the trophies or the win-loss record. These benefits include but are not limited to:

- The opportunity to introduce yourself to your *real* self.
- The development of physical and emotional fitness.
- The development of teamwork and friendships (some life-long).
- Learning how to lose with dignity and win with humility.
- The establishment of perseverance in difficulty.
- Learning to overcome adversity.

Following are ten key aspects to keep in mind when planning to move to the next level athletically.

1-Listen and Respect Your Coaches

Your coaches give extra sets of eyes and ears and possess wisdom to help you make adjustments to your training and game plan. They have experience and knowledge that will give you what you need to succeed. They have the advantage of looking at you and your opponent from a different view point which will help you as you compete.

As an athlete, you are looking at the task before you, (a goal or an opponent) much like a mountain climber views a mountain. It stands in front of you large and imposing. But a coach looks at the same task (the goal or opponent) like one who is in a helicopter or plane. He sees the same mountain from a completely different point of view and gives a unique perspective to the task ahead. Listen to the ones who see things from a better vantage point.

2-Respect Your Opponent

Respect for your opponent causes you to prepare properly. The list is long and ever-growing of teams and individuals who took the talent of their opponents too lightly and were surprised and defeated. During the contest it is equally important to act respectfully with your opponent. It is entirely possible to be a victor without victims. This has everything to do with how you treat those you are competing against. Speaking respectfully to them and about them will gain the respect of the fans on both sides of the competition. Furthermore, running up the score is both disrespectful and unnecessary and may come back on you at a later meeting.

3-Eat Well

Food is the fuel your body will use to help you perform optimally. Just as your car needs the correct fuel, your body needs the right food. The key is to avoid *zero calorie* foods that would give little energy. The proper foods are those that will help you build muscle and provide for muscle fibers to contract strongly and repeatedly.

4-Determine to Outwork Your Opposition

When you don't work hard and your opponent does, it gives them the advantage. There are lots of things outside of your control. Your opponent's size, speed, numbers, and facilities are things you can do nothing about. But your preparation is completely within your control. Doing what you are told will make you good. Doing more than what you are told will develop greatness. No one can achieve greatness until he is willing to endure the pain it takes to get to the top.

5-Develop a Solid Game Plan

Your game plan should put you in the best position to win. This should include what you want to do along with what you will do in response to changes in the game or competition. Your plan should maximize the skills you have at your disposal but must be flexible enough to make adjustments as the contest unfolds.

Studying and understanding your opponent's strengths and weaknesses as well as your own will give you the edge you need to do your best.

6-Choose a Sport That You Enjoy

For those who are looking to become involved in athletics, some things should be considered. Athletics should be enjoyed. That is the main purpose of participation. A sport should be chosen with fun being the main motivation. The sport should also be accessible. Downhill skiing in Indiana, or surfing in Ohio are obvious poor choices. Along with this, those who live in the inner city will have little access to sports like golf and hockey.

Along with accessibility, the sport should be affordable. This is where a person's budget comes into play. Participation in some sports are much less expensive than others. To play basketball, you need shoes, shorts and a ball. Beyond running shoes and shorts, little is needed to compete in road races. Other sports, however, are very expensive. Golf and football are two examples. If the right sport is chosen, great enjoyment can be had through involvement in athletics.

Safety counts! Make sure you are practicing and competing safely! Some sports require very little to ensure safety like golf, basketball, or running. Others need special equipment to help the participant participate in a safe manner such as football, shooting, boxing, and to a lesser degree, baseball. When safety is assured, athletes can play with a total commitment to the sport.

7-Accept the Pain and Sacrifice of Improvement

There is intrinsic pain associated with improvement. Some of the pain is internal. Sacrificing social freedom and pushing past physical pain barriers are two examples. Some pain is external such as receiving a blow in boxing or being tackled in football. Regardless of where the pain comes from, it comes as a result of participation and training.

With training and competition comes internal and external pain. You must be willing to embrace the pain if you are going to improve!

8-Help Those Around You Improve

If you are on a team you have teammates. If you are in an individual sport, you have others around whom you can help improve. The higher you go in your sport, the broader the influence you will have. Commit to their improvement and the team will get better. Individually, you will reap the internal benefits of helping those around you.

NFL hall of famer, Jerry Rice is a great example of this. Although not required, many years he attended *rookie camp*. He trained right alongside the younger players and helped them become better athletes. The team's accomplishments (three super bowl championships) speak for themselves and there is no denying that he had a big part in it.

9-Become a Student of Your Sport

Every sport is packed with rules, techniques, and history. As an athlete, you must commit to total involvement in each of these areas. Knowing the history of your sport and the stories of great performers and performances will motivate you to be the best. Understanding the rules is a basic requirement of participation. Researching the latest technological advances and training techniques will help you reach your greatest potential.

You must keep up with the changes that happen in your sport. Rules are constantly evolving. Football is a good example of this. It is no longer legal to lead with your head down when you tackle. If a field goal is missed and is caught by an opposing player in the field of play, he can run the ball back for a touchdown (see Auburn vs. Alabama-2013). In college, if a player is down inside the field of play, the clock stops momentarily when a first down is made but starts immediately upon the referee spotting the ball down.

New techniques and equipment are developing regularly. Plates instead of spokes in biking, oversized drivers in golf, strength development programs, GPS trackers in football helmets, nutritional advances, and new types of poles in the pole vault are examples of these.

You must stay on top of these subjects in order to see your best personal results.

10-Compete According to the Rules

There isn't much satisfaction in showing off a medal or trophy if it is obtained by dishonest means. The rules are in place to ensure that the contest is played fairly by each side. Knowing the rules and committing to abiding by them is a basic component of any sport.

In recent history, we have seen the violation of rules ending in the reputation of the participants being scarred. In 2015, The New England Patriots were found guilty of playing with under-inflated footballs. In 1980, Rosie Ruez falsely won the Boston Marathon. Lance Armstrong has been stripped of his victories in the Tour De France due to blood doping. Mike Tyson lost the title fight to Evander Holyfield due to biting Holyfield's ear and there is an ever-growing list of athletes who are suspended for use of performance enhancing drugs.

Knowing and abiding by the rules is a basic principle of all athletics. A victory achieved the right way builds a memory that cannot be taken or replaced.

Embracing the ten key points mentioned above will enable you to enjoy all the benefits involvement in athletics can bring. These benefits will last far beyond your years of competition and training and will go a long way toward a fulfilling and rewarding experience.

- 8 -
Steps to Fulfilling Worship

"But an hour is coming, and now is, when the true worshipers will worship the Father in spirit and truth; for such people the Father seeks to be His worshipers." John 4:23

Proskuneo (Pros-kee-neh-o) is the Greek word for worship. It means to kiss. When applied to the worship of God, it means to kiss toward God. That is to say that worship is the act of romancing God. On human terms, when we romance someone, we are involved in activities that will draw their attention and demonstrate honor toward them. We spend time with them. We talk with them. We change our behavior to please them. This is no different than what we strive to do in the worship of God. In worshipping Him we are ascribing "Worth-ship" to Him.

But, as Chuck Swindoll so aptly points out, "We are so caught up in our activities that we tend to worship our work, work at our play, and play at our worship."

But when we engage in the true worship of God, and we in fact, worship Him "in spirit and in truth," we find that we gain the benefits and He receives the glory.

So, what are the aspects of worship in which we should be involved in? Are there practices we should pursue as we seek to honor the Lord in our worship? The answer is *Yes*, and following are some key points worth considering.

1-Regularly Engage in Personal and Corporate Worship

Nike would tell us, "Just do it!" The worship of God is a decision. Whether you are alone, or with others you must make a decision to worship on the soul level. Attending a worship service or putting aside personal worship time must be intentional.

The story is told of a grandson that relayed to his grandfather that he was no longer interested in going to church because he didn't see the benefit. The wise grandfather did not react immediately. Instead he nodded and handed him an old and dirty coal bucket with instructions to fill it from the well. The boy complied but when he walked back to his grand-father he found the bucket empty. The grandfather instructed him to go back and return again. The result was the same. Two more times he was directed to the well and two more times he returned with an empty bucket. Finally, the exasperated boy complained that it was no use. The bucket had too many holes in it to hold water. The grandfather agreed but drew the boy's attention to the inside of the bucket which was now clean. The water did not stay in, but the effect was to clean the bucket. Even if you don't *feel* the effects, regular intentional worship has an impact. *Soul cleansing* can happen even when you don't realize it.

2-Come to Worship Expectantly

You may feel, "I didn't get anything out of that worship time." The ensuing question is, "What did you bring to get it in?" You cannot expect God to pour into your life when you are not open to receive it. It is not possible to fill a full vessel. Jer. 29:13 says, "You will seek me and find me when you search for me with all your heart."

Change your attitude from, "We *have* to go to church" to "We *get* to go to church!" and you may find the Spirit of God entering into your heart in a new way.

3-Come to Worship Cleanly

Too often a family will argue all the way to the worship campus and then somehow turn on *the worship switch* when the car touches the parking lot. Then they wonder why the effects of their time in worship is less than desired.

Whether alone or with the church family, coming cleanly should be the prerequisite for a worshipful experience. This means searching your heart and confessing any offenses you may be carrying. Coming cleanly means you are bringing a clean heart for God to write on and a clean mind for Him to speak to.

4-Prepare for Worship the Night Before

When you are prepared for worship the night before, you minimize frustrations, emotions, and a harried attitude. With clothes laid out, breakfast planned, and the family in bed at a responsible hour, the next morning can be engaged with much less anxiety and struggle. Whether leaving for dinner or a movie, people naturally make preparations to arrive on time, and with an appetite and attitude to fully enjoy the experience. This should be no different when the day of corporate worship arrives.

5-Minimize Distractions

While alone, turn the Television and radio off and silence your phone. In a corporate setting, sit close to the front and do your best to ignore those around you who can be a distraction.

The acrostic F.O.C.U.S. stands for Forcing Ourselves to Concentrate Upon the Savior. With this in mind, you can better develop an open and thankful heart receptive to an encounter with God.

6-Develop a Style of Prayer

This is not a suggestion to engage in rote memory or repetition. Jesus spoke against that in Matt. 6:7, "And when you pray, do not keep on babbling like pagans, for they think they will be heard because of their many words.

However, in Matt. 6:9-13 Jesus instructs us, "This, then, is how you should pray: Our Father in heaven, hallowed be your name, your kingdom come, your will be done, on earth as it is in heaven. Give us today our daily bread. And forgive us our debts, as we also have forgiven our debtors. And lead us not into temptation but deliver us from the evil one."

This is a pattern of prayer that Jesus gives His followers. Closer examination shows us that the prayer starts with praise, moves to His will being done, a request for provision, and forgiveness of sins along with strength to resist temptation.

Another pattern of prayer is done by using the acrostic A.C.T.S.
A-Adoration
C-Confession
T-Thanksgiving
S-Supplication

7-Be Authentic in Your Worship Style

While on vacation, a man visited a nearby church. When the preacher made a comment he liked, he responded with "Amen!" This was met by several stares from those around him. Soon he shouted, "That's right!" and heard several shushes. Not able to restrain himself later he shouted, "Praise the Lord!" This was followed by an usher telling him to be quiet or he would be asked to leave. He informed the man, "I can't help it. I got the Spirit in me!" The man looked at him and said, "Well, you didn't get it here, so be quiet!"

Just as there are different personalities, there are different styles of worship. Some are vocal. Some are introspective. Some shed tears easily. Whatever your style, be authentic before the one who knows you completely and allow others to express themselves according to their personality and preference.

8-Keep a Prayer Journal

As you spend time in prayer and worship, write down what you are praying about, particularly the requests that are made. This way, when the Lord meets your need, you are in a better position to offer up praise during your worship time. If there is a special verse that resonates with you, you can also jot it down along with the date it hit home with you and label it, "PPP" which stands for *Pure, Precious, Promise*.

9-Study the Topic of Worship

The word of God is replete with references to worship. Among many types of worship, altars were built, songs were sung, sacrifices were made, and prayers were offered. When you get a clear glimpse of the character of God you will naturally find yourself in a state of worship. The character of God is openly reveled in the names of God. Among the many names of God, we find:
- Jehovah Jireh: *The Lord is my provider*
- Jehovah Raphe: *The one who heals*
- Elohim: *Creator God*
- Jehovah Nisse: *The Lord is my banner*
- El Roy: *The one who sees*

He's the good shepherd, the living water, the alpha and omega, the bread of life, the door, the one who was, and is, and is to come. Seeing the hand of God, compels you to worship at the feet of God.

10-See Worship as a Lifestyle

Too many followers of Christ see their lives divided into two distinct categories: *sacred* and *secular*. In the sacred category they find themselves in church, Bible study, prayer, and fellowship with other believers. In the secular box they are at home, on vacation, at school, or conducting business.

But the life of a Christian is to be lived as a sacred life, all the time and everywhere! There is NO secular side. Everything you do, say, and think is to be an act of worship. In Gal. 2:20, Paul states it this way, "I have been crucified with Christ and I no longer live, but Christ lives in me. The life I now live in the body, I live by faith in the Son of God, who loved me and gave himself for me."

Besides their inevitable death, there are two main things that all those who have been crucified have in common: They cannot see behind them, and they have no plans of their own. This is a description of a life of surrender. This is what it means to be totally committed to Christ. This is a picture of a lifestyle of worship.

Worshipping Him *in Spirit and in truth* means being enveloped in an attitude of ascribing *worth-ship* to Him. Both in the personal setting as well as the corporate setting, an encounter with God can be experienced when a person's heart is clean, and open to this spiritual adventure.

- 9 -
Steps to Establishing an Overcomer's Life

Everyone wants to be known as an overcomer. Public opinion and personal satisfaction are great for those who have met obstacles in life and have come out on the victor's side. Meeting adversity head-on and engaging in the battle births tremendous confidence and lasting satisfaction. Following are important ingredients to launch you in the direction of living an overcomer's life. Put these in place and you'll be well on your way to establishing yourself as an overcomer.

1-Don't Let Anything Beat You That Doesn't Have a Heart

This is simply about determination. *Grit* is a word that is commonly used to describe a determined person. It simply means that you have an attitude that won't allow circumstances, emotions, desires, or feelings stop you.

You'll find that most times, your biggest opponent is not the person or team you're competing against. The biggest obstacle to victory comes from within. What are some of the things that don't have a heart? Pain, fatigue, discouragement, confusion, distractions, scoreboards, attitudes, numbers, noise, and time, to name a few.

You must be determined not to let these things stop you. Preparation, mental toughness, concentration, physical conditioning, and a proper attitude are some of the *antidotes* that will off-set the things that will get between you and victory.

2-Work Hard

Hard work pays off. Most times working hard gives you the results you desire by way of a pay check or trophy. But there are some clear

benefits to working hard that go beyond your bank account or the winner's platform.
1. Working hard gives you confidence. When you are prepared, you can participate knowing that you did your best and are in position to succeed.
2. Working hard gives you a great sense of accomplishment. Knowing that you have done what it takes to prepare you for the task ahead simply gives you a good feeling. Preparation itself involves overcoming obstacles so you are in a sense already winning small battles on your way to the *big battle*.
3. Working hard lets you know you belong. When you work hard, and you know that others on your team have worked hard it builds a sense of team camaraderie that cannot be obtained simply by talking about it.
4. Working hard prepares you for future difficulties which may not even be related to the present task or competition. When you have overcome a great obstacle, lesser challenges are handled with less trepidation. For instance, if you have run a marathon, a 5K does not intimidate you. Likewise, if you have given a presentation before the company's executives, teaching a class of emergency preparedness does not bother you.

3-Decompress

The tachometer in a car is used to tell the number of RPMs (rounds per minute) the engine is putting out. When the needle gets to a certain point (the red line) you know that you should shift to a higher gear. Over time, failure to do so could blow your engine.

Similarly, when you maintain a high stress level in your life, physically, mentally, or emotionally, and you keep the *needle* pegged there, you could suffer an injury on some level. Some call this *burn out*. Something has to give.

Knowing when you are *red lining* it is essential to good health. You must be wise enough to understand when it is time to back off and decompress. Taking a break from pressure will give your body and mind the time it needs to recover so you can re-enter the contest.

4-Learn What Energizes You

Just as decompressing is important, knowing what re-fuels or energizes you (physically or emotionally) is key to re-entering the competition. This is where knowing yourself comes in.

Many believe erroneously, that the difference between an introvert and extrovert is seen in how they behave publicly. While this may give some indication, it may not be completely accurate. There are numerous examples of people who look like introverts because of how we see them publicly or professionally but in reality, they are introverts. Teachers, preachers, politicians, law enforcement, and others may give us the idea that they are extroverts, but until we see them privately, we won't have a clear understanding of what category they fit.

So how do we determine if we are an extrovert or introvert so we can know how to re-charge our physical and emotional batteries? The answer is found in how we spend our free time when we are drained or worn out. An extrovert is more likely to lean toward activities that involve action or people. Going to a party, playing a sport, or even seeing an action movie may be just the release this type of person needs. Conversely, being alone, reading a book, or sitting quietly listening to relaxing music would appeal to the introvert.

Along with knowing into which category you fit, is knowing how much of a re-charge you need. Just as there are two different charges for a battery, (trickle charge and quick charge), there are different types of charges we need. Sometimes it's a few hours strolling along in a park or sitting by the fire that will put things right emotionally for the introvert. A pick-up game of basketball may do it for the extrovert. These are examples of quick charges.

At other times, a trickle charge is needed. These are longer periods of release and disengagement that are called for. A two-week vacation filled with sight-seeing, hiking, and visiting family are what extroverts long for. Several days at home (*a staycation*) working on projects or sitting at the beach with family may be just the ticket for the introvert.

5-Develop Lasting Friendships

Years ago, the phrase was coined, *Love makes the world go 'round.* Since then, another phrase was added coupled with that phrase and instructing us further, *Love doesn't make the world go 'round, it makes the trip worth-while.*

It's all about relationships! You were not meant to live this live in isolation. Each life touches another and has an impact. We are social beings meant to be involved on some level with each other. Yet the average American male over thirty years of age does not have one close friend (besides his wife) that he can share his hopes, dreams, fears, and disappointments. This simply should not be!

The type of relationships we should have are symbiotic in nature. It means that we each have things that when shared, can be equally beneficial. Some call it a *win-win relationship*. Put another way, it means, *I need you and I need to feel needed by you.*

Developing deep friendships means that you must be *friend-worthy*. That is to say you must develop traits that will cause others to be drawn to you and desire to be your friend. How is this done? Following are five simple and easily developed attributes of good friends:

1. Time. You must commit to spending time with others sharing experiences that are mutually enjoyable.
2. A Sympathetic Ear. Becoming a good listener who is willing to allow others to share without judgment or input is a catalyst to a good friendship.
3. Resources. Generous people are always attractive. An open hand is as valuable as an open ear.
4. Availability. A good friend is someone who comes in when the rest of the world is walking out. When needed you always show up. *A friend in need is a friend indeed!*
5. Trust. One who can keep a secret and take information *to the grave* will always be highly valued. We only befriend those who we trust.

The good news is each of these attributes of friendship are yours if you are willing to put forth the effort. Lasting friendships are available if you will do what it takes to become *friend-worthy*.

6-Develop the Character Traits You Admire

All of us see things in others that we admire. Loyalty, a strong work ethic, wisdom, humor, generosity, determination, faith, kindness, and sincerity are just a few of them. How did those who carry those traits get them? Is it inbred in them? Did they seek them out? Is it just a part of their personality? Some of each of these may be true, but equally true is the idea that these traits can be obtained by intentionally choosing them.

When you see a trait in someone else, write it down and make an effort to adopt that into your own personality. You do this by a conscious decision to exhibit that trait at least once that day. You might even develop a quick plan on how you will demonstrate it. If you want to become generous, put aside some of your money or possessions and come up with a name of one you will share it with that day.

If it's determination you want to have as a part of your personality, find something small to overcome that day. Perhaps you want to adopt kindness as a way of life for yourself. Look for ways to demonstrate that today.

If you will set your sights on the attributes you want to be noted for, and practice them regularly, they will become a part of you and others will readily see those positive character traits in you.

7-Ask for Advice and Help

None of us is as strong as all of us! This is a law of life that no one is excluded from. Different viewpoints, ideas, opinions, and experiences can all be a great benefit to us. Sometimes what's needed is an extra hand or additional muscle fibers to get the task completed. The saying, "Many hands make light work" is true.

The enemy of seeking help is pride. Too often we don't ask for help because we've decided that it would make us look weak or less intelligent. If we would overcome our pride and ask for help or advice, we can side-step some of the problems that come about by trying to do everything alone. Someone has said, "If I'm the smartest person in the room, I'm in the wrong room." This comes from a one who is comfortable with the idea that they don't know it all and is willing to admit that there are others who have more knowledge or experience. This person is comfortable with asking for help from others and is most likely to complete at task with more ease, speed, and enjoyment.

8-Invest Yourself in People or Causes

Albert Schweitzer once said, "The only ones among you who will be really happy are those who will have sought and found how to serve." You must get outside yourself and the *me-ism* mentality that is so often touted by our society. Find something or someone that you believe in and give yourself to the effort of making it, or them, better. Perhaps it's fighting cancer or bigotry or meeting the needs of the poor. Maybe you desire to have an impact on a young or old person's life. You may want to invest your efforts in the environment or the plight of the homeless. Whatever your passion is, sell out to making a difference!

Tom Bodett is quoted as saying, "They say a person needs just three things to be truly happy in this world: someone to love, something to do, and something to hope for." You'll find that making a difference in a cause or a person's life will make a great difference in your own. Investing yourself in people or causes is one ingredient you need to add to your personal recipe for a fulfilling life.

9-Set Goals

No matter how old you are, there are still things you can reach for. Setting and achieving goals is vitally important to getting what you want or helping you get where you want to go. Setting and achieving goals:

A. Puts your desires in focus.
B. Helps you achieve more.
C. Gives you great satisfaction.
D. Helps you discover what's really important to you.
E. Gives you a story worth sharing.
F. Builds confidence.

When developing goals, a key aspect is choosing something that excites you. It needs to be something that *you* want to do. This is not something others think you should do. This is something you desire. It comes from within. If the goal does not fill you with passion, you may lose interest and turn to something else.

Also, your goals need to be concrete. They must be things that can be measured. Losing weight may be desirable, but you must list the amount of weight you want to lose in order to see when you have reached that particular goal.

Furthermore, you must put a deadline to your goal. You have to have a date in which you wish to achieve what you are reaching for. If you do not attach a deadline to your goal, you will leave it open-ended and you will never get to the point where you can say, "I reached my goal."

After a time of celebrating the reaching of a particular goal, you must now turn your attention to the next goal. Dwelling on past accomplishments should only be used to propel you to the next.

A young man moved into his college dorm as a freshman. Among the things he unpacked was a large brass *V*. He tacked that letter on his door and moved it with him when he moved from dorm to dorm. No matter where he moved, one of the first things he attached to his door was that *V*. Though many asked him what the letter stood for, he never shared the answer with them. The answer however was revealed on the day of graduation when he was announced as the class valedictorian. His academic goal was accomplished!

When your life is framed by goal setting, you'll find that you have achieved more than you ever thought possible.

10-Become an Expert at Something

When you have great understanding about a particular subject it gives you deep confidence to speak in small and even large groups. The feeling of self-assurance you gain will be well worth the effort it takes to get you there.

In order to achieve this however, you must be willing to do what it takes to gain the knowledge you will need in a specific area. This will take time and effort on your part and a clear commitment to the subject you have chosen. Some important elements must be in place in order for you to pursue this endeavor.

You must choose something about which you have a passion. The topic or subject must ignite within you a strong urge to know and pursue more. This passion will motivate you to begin a relentless hunt to capture information and knowledge.

You must place yourself in the presence of someone who has mastered the subject. This is one who is universally known as an expert. Time with them, asking questions, sitting in on lectures, and conversation will automatically increase your knowledge.

You also must become a reader. More than ever, information is available to those who are willing to seek it. It could be in book form, or on-line. The wealth of knowledge is there for the taking.

Beyond this, you may need to enlist in formal instruction. This could be in a traditional classroom, through an on-line program, or in some type of hybrid program.

You'll find that the time, money, and effort it takes to corner the market on a particular area of interest will be well worth what it cost to inculcate the knowledge to be had and the resulting confidence and fulfillment it gives.

- 10 -
Steps to Building a Hall-of-Fame Life

A husband was about to attend a banquet honoring him as the town's man of the year. All week long he talked about it and peppered his conversation with comments about it. While getting dressed for the event he asked his wife, "How many really great men do you think there are in this town?"

Putting her hands on her hips and giving a heavy sigh she replied, "I Not sure how many there are but I'm certain there's one less than you think there is!"

A few days before the *Hall of Fame* banquet, I referenced the evening and said to my wife, "Wow! Think about all that's gone on in my life! I've traveled all over the world. I've written several books. I lead an incredible church. I've earned three masters and a doctorate. And now I'm being inducted into my high school's athletic hall of fame. In all your wildest dreams, did you ever think that something like this could happen to a guy like me?" My wife turned to me, smiled and said, "Oh sweetie. You're not in my wildest dreams!"

Leave it to a spouse to put things into perspective. Obviously the above is a short note of humor. But the message behind it is one that will carry us well. No matter where athletics has taken you, it is vitally important to keep things in perspective. Wins, losses, pain, elation, disappointments, anticipation, and experience must all be kept in their proper place if you are going to gain all the benefits of participation.

I was able to compete in competitive athletics until the age of twenty-six. Beyond that, I also coached for a number of years. So, I spent a good part of my life as an athlete, coach, and fan. A life of athletics has been so good to me. I have made friends, enjoyed victories, learned to take defeat with dignity, traveled all over the U.S. and parts of Europe, developed a strong work ethic, exercised discipline, and built a genuine respect for authority. But beyond the athletic world, athletics has held me in good stead. I gleaned wisdom from participation in sports that I have been able to apply to so many areas of my life. Following are four monumental lessons a life of athletics has taught me. I am convinced that these *pillars* will help hold you up as well.

1-Nothing Great Has Ever Been Done Without Enthusiasm, But Enthusiasm Without Direction Leads to Disaster

The story is told of a man who met another man working for a large corporation.

"How long have you been working here?" he asked.

The second man gave a heavy sigh and said, "Since the day they threatened to fire me!"

Attending the work place and going to work are not the same thing. Employers expect us to put some energy behind the tasks we're assigned coupled with a good attitude.

The sign above the door of a factory reads, "If you're not fired with enthusiasm, you will be fired with enthusiasm."

A close friend of mine worked for a good-sized manufacturer. He'd been working there for about a year and felt it was time to ask for a raise. One day he worked up the nerve to approach the owner of the company with the request for an increase in pay. The owner listened to his request and replied. "I agree that it's time to give you a raise. And your raise will become effective when you do."

It's not enough to attend the work place physically. Those in whose charge we are expect us to be there with our mind as well as our body. They are looking for us to commit to making the company better and to help them take it to the next level.

Bob Richards was a three-time Olympic athlete in two events-the pole vault and decathlon. He sums up the need for commitment this way:

> *If a man is going to be what he ought to be, he's got to be willing to put out just a little bit more. There isn't a gigantic difference between victory or defeat: More often it is simply by the smallest margin that a man is named the winner.*

The difference between a Ph.D. in school and the fellow who didn't quite make it is that little bit more study, that extra page that a man turns every night as he burns the midnight oil. It's that extra lap around the track, that extra five minutes a person puts into his workout, into his school work, or into his home life that makes the difference in his life.

There is no question that enthusiasm makes a tremendous difference in a person's life. But unbridled enthusiasm can lead to horrific results. This is seen in the example of the way Eskimos rid themselves of wolves that threaten their livestock. To kill a wolf, a man will take a razor-sharp knife and place it in a container with the sharpened end facing up. He then will fill the container with blood from a slaughtered animal completely covering the blade. Left outside for a few hours, the blood will freeze. Next, he'll put the block of ice in the path of the wolf. The wolf will come upon it and begin licking it. As he continues licking it, his tongue will freeze and become numb. This keeps him from feeling the pain of the knife cutting his tongue. The taste of blood heightens his excitement and he will cut his tongue almost completely off which eventually will lead to his death. The unrestrained enthusiasm of the wolf brings destruction to the beast. It is the same with us if we don't learn to channel out enthusiasm.

From a personal stand-point, I learned this lesson my sophomore year in high school. As a freshman I was anything but fast. But through hard work, maturity, and puberty, I gained the speed I needed to be a good running back. So, when the season started that sophomore year, I found myself in the starting position on the Junior Varsity squad. During one particular practice we were doing a drill on the freshman soccer field. The defense was on the other side of the seven-man sled. They would fire-out and hit the sled and then pursue around it to catch the running backs.

We ran the option and it was my job to catch the pitch and make the defense catch me. The sled was set up so that the running backs would be going through the center of the soccer goal (without the net). As the sled would invariably turn, we would adjust our alignment.

On one particular snap I took off running. I ran as hard as I could, looked for the pitch, felt the ball hit my hands and my body hit the goal post. I never saw the hit coming. I just knew that I was down with lots of pain in several areas of my body. My metal face-mask was bent, my shoulder pads were creased, and I developed a long and deep bruise on my chest. The lesson of keeping your eye on the ball took on new meaning for me that day. The bigger lesson was, run hard but keep an eye on where you're going.

Enthusiasm is a necessary asset, but you must counter your excitement with proper perspective and direction.

2-You Must Develop an Unwavering Commitment to Excellence

The journey to the top of any endeavor always carries with it the potential to be painful in any number of ways. But no one can achieve greatness until he is willing to hurt himself deeply. The pursuit of excellence means a commitment not to settle for anything less than your absolute best regardless of the time or effort needed

I was only a young boy when my dad instilled this in me. We were working in his shop on a project for the scouts. My job was to sand (by hand) a piece of wood that was to go under a table. Because it was going to be hidden, I didn't see the need to put much effort into getting it completely smooth. I was more concerned with moving on to the next task and finishing the project. My dad picked up the wood and looked at me. I knew what he was thinking and jumped into his stare with the comment, "It's gonna be under the table. No one's gonna see it." My dad's eyes never left me. He said, "Your fingerprints are on everything you do." Then he added the words that have stayed with me and guided me my entire life, "Doing it right beats doing it over."

Perhaps you've bought a new pair of slacks recently. It is not uncommon to find a small typewritten note in the pocket of your new purchase. It might read, "This garment inspected by inspector #24." That is a call to excellence. It demonstrates that the garment has been examined and calls inspector #24 to take responsibility for the quality of the clothing. There is always an increase in quality when accountability is involved.

Along with accountability comes a personal involvement in the task. If you have a personal connection to the job you are doing, you automatically *raise the bar* of your effort. It simply means more to you because you have a personal stake in the task.

This was seen during WWII in a particular factory saddled with the task of sewing parachutes. Above the door in bold letters was a sign reading, "This chute may be worn by your husband or son." Naturally the personal investment drove these workers to put their all into the effort. The thought of someone they loved wearing the chute they were working on motivated those ladies to settle for nothing less than their best.

The level of the quality of a job lasts well beyond the job itself. A person may pick up the product, but you are the one left with the memory of the effort you put into it. If a task does not call for excellence perhaps it doesn't call at all!

3-You Can Be a Victor Without Any Victims

Winning is a wonderful thing! I enjoy winning as much as anyone. But over the years, athletics has taught me that there is a way to win that makes victory all the more enjoyable.

During the 1980's there was a great push in our country built around the concept of selfishness. It was an era of *Me-ism*. It was about putting yourself first and climbing on everyone else to get to the top. There was even a best-seller titled, "Taking Care of #1." But it didn't take long before people noticed just how empty the climb can be and how lonely it was at the top. That was due largely to the fact that those at the top realized that they climbed alone.

There is nothing wrong with doing your best and getting to the top but the view from the top is so much clearer and better when you take others with you.

Wright Patman was a congressman from Texas. He died in 1976. At his funeral, the comment was made of him, "He rose up mighty high, but he brung us all up with him." Here was a man who climbed the political ladder of success, but he did it in such a way that others were able to climb with him.

Of course, in your effort to win, others have to lose. But the way you win doesn't have to make them feel like losers. It's called *Respect*. The respect you have for the competition will be seen in how you carry yourself in the time leading up to the competition as well as during the competition itself. Three key mandates are involved in this:

1. Prepare your hardest. You cannot control the size, number, or condition of opponents. You have nothing to do with their preparation or facilities. But your preparation is the one thing that is completely under your control. How much you study,

train, and work to get yourself ready to compete is up to you.
2. Don't talk disparagingly about them. If you put your opponent down with ridiculing comments four things will happen: You will motivate them. You will begin believing your comments and cut your preparation short. You will look bad to the public. Your victory will not be seen as great because after all, they weren't that good. It is possible to talk publicly with confidence without being critical of those you will face.
3. Lose with grace and win with humility. In athletics as well as life you will lose at times and you will win at other times. You must learn to do both with a level of class that keeps everything in perspective. When you lose, evaluate what went wrong and determine to correct your mistakes. Hold your head high, congratulate your opponent and tell yourself you will rise above this loss. When you win, keep your head high and your voice low. Enjoy every minute of your success but continue to keep things in perspective.

I was privileged to learn to be a victor without victims during my high school days. Competition in the pole vault can last beyond the entire meet. So, hours are spent around the same people. When that happens, you have a great opportunity to get to know the other athletes. It was during these times that I made great friends with the other vaulters. We helped each other with the standards, catching poles, marking steps, and encouraging each other. Winning was a priority, but relationships were not destroyed in the process. I even had some of the other vaulters come by during school and pick me up so we could sneak into the field house at West Point and practice together.

During one particular football game, I remember getting picked up off the ground from a linebacker I was friends with at a rival high school. There is no question that he hit me as hard as he could and stopped me cold (when he could catch me) but then he would grab my hand and lift me to my feet for another play. On one down it seemed like I was under their entire team. I heard a man yelling "Get off him! Get off him!" I thought it was the official but found myself face to face with my linebacker friend.

Making yourself into a winner does not necessarily mean you have to make others *losers*!

4-Take What You Do Seriously, But Don't Take Yourself Too Seriously

In competitive poker there is a point when you witness a player risking all he has on one Individual hand. The player puts his cards face-down on the table, slides all his chips to the center, and declares, "All in!" There is no turning back. It represents total commitment. So much of life calls for serious attention. A call to excellence is a call to serious application. You must be *all in* if you are going to reach your fullest potential. The word "FOCUS" stands for Forcing Ourselves to Concentrate Upon the Subject. This means a total release of all you are into all you do and is a necessary component to becoming the best.

But if you do not build in time away from *the fight* you risk experiencing damage at the core level of your being. The adage is true, "The bow that is always bent, will someday break." In athletics, the key is to be mentally engaged but physically relaxed. This will enable you to maintain your competitive edge without completely draining your physical resources.

In life, you must find a way to disengage from the stress and pressures of work, study, and advancement in order to re-load and re-tool for productivity over the long haul. This is called decompression. Boilers have a built-in pressure release valve in order to avoid destroying the equipment when too much pressure is built up. If the pressure inside the system gets too high a valve opens up, releases steam, and brings the pressure down. Decompression in life, means finding your own pressure release valve so you don't blow a *gasket* and suffer loss.

It is vital that you find some sort of distraction that will pull you away mentally from the intensity of your tasks. Some develop hobbies such as knitting, yard work, writing, or wood crafts. Others escape the pressure by a change in scenery. Boating, hiking, or exercising are excellent ways to remove yourself from the point of pressure.

Laughter is great decompressor. It is a natural way of disengaging yourself from the pressure of the struggle. It's good for your heart and circular system, emotionally settles you, and may even make you easier to live with.

Personally, I try to laugh every day. And so often the subject of my humor is myself. In the south we have a saying, "Get over yourself!" This is another way of saying, "Lighten up! Don't take yourself so seriously!"

Intentional Steps: The Pathway to Better Living

During my senior year in high school, I was under a great deal of pressure athletically. I was one of the top vaulters in the state and was heading for the county and sectional championships, which would lead to the state level.

One day, I was leaving the cafeteria and walking down the short hall to the gym. On the left was a long trophy case. When I walked by, I noticed something that immediately caught my eye. It was a large poster on the inside of the glass with my picture on it. The picture was one that was taken in second grade (my mother supplied it). In bold letters the poster read, "Congratulations to Steve Jirgal-Regional qualifier for the Howdy Doody look-a-like contest. Best of luck in Provo Utah!" It was obvious that the coaches were having a great time at my expense.

At first, I was embarrassed and maybe a little angry. But before I reached the gym and the circle of coaches waiting on my entrance, I decided to join them in the humor of it all. There was no question that I took what I was doing very seriously, but that moment called for me not to take myself too seriously. The humor and distraction were just what I needed.

This ability to laugh at myself carried on to adulthood. Several years ago, I suffered with a serious bout of diverticulitis. I was in great pain due to a perforated colon. Urgent surgery was called for. The morning of the attack found me in the emergency room waiting attention. I was given morphine to relieve the pain and was to await a visit from a surgeon.

When they learned of my situation, some wonderful friends worked their way to my bedside. After a short visit, nature called, and I requested some privacy. After emptying my bladder, a humorous idea hit me. I gently made my way to the sink and filled the plastic jug up to the top. Then I placed it on the tray in front of me and waited for my wife and friends to return. I said nothing as they came into the room but broke out in laughter when I saw their eyes focus on the completely filled bottle. If you can't laugh when morphine does its job, you can't laugh at all!

One day a few years ago I noticed I was having trouble seeing out of my right eye. Tests revealed that I had a brain tumor. The tumor was sitting on my pituitary gland and was pressing on my optic nerve. Surgery was scheduled shortly.

Steps to Building a Hall-of-Fame Life

When I met with the doctor to discuss the surgical procedure, I explained to him that putting me to sleep was very important. But it was more important that the medical crew wake me up. So, I told him that to ensure that, I would tell them the front part of a joke just before they put me under. The deal was, that if they wanted to hear the punch-line they would have to wake me back up. (There is even humor in thinking that humor would be the motivation that they needed).

As planned, just before they wheeled me into the O.R. I called for their attention and began telling them an appropriate joke. I explained:

> "A man went into a diner and saw a pirate seated at a nearby table. He wore a large black hat, had a peg leg, a hook for a hand, and a patch on his eye. The man kept glancing at the pirate but before long could not contain his curiosity. So, he approached the pirate and said, 'Are you a real pirate?' The man answered and said, 'Aye! I'm a real pirate.' The man asked, 'How did you get the wooden leg?' The pirate answered, 'I was fightin' on the deck when a cannon ball came and took off me leg, so I had to get this peg.'
>
> 'Well, how did you wind up with a hook for a hand?' the man asked.
>
> 'I was fightin' a lad and he came across with his sword and took off me hand, so I had to get me a hook' the pirate answered.
>
> 'Wow!' the man said. 'And how did you lose your eye and need a patch?'

This is where I stopped the joke leading to motivating them to wake me up for the punch line. The punch line goes:

> The pirate said, 'I was up on the deck and a seagull flew over and pooped right in me eye!'
>
> The man was surprised and asked, 'You mean you lost your eye from seagull poop?'

'No!' The pirate said. 'First day with me hook!'

Now that is not where the humor ends. When I was in recovery the surgeon came in and explained that everything went well and that I should have a full recovery. He finished and asked if I had any questions. I didn't and told him so. Then I asked him if he had any questions for me. "Why would I have any questions for you?" he asked. I said, "Well, don't you want to hear the punchline of the joke?"

Then he surprised me by saying, "You already told us the punchline." He explained, "I've never seen anything like it. We were bringing you up out of the anesthesia and you started talking. You told the punchline to the entire staff. Everyone was laughing."

Laughter tears rimmed my wife's eyes. She shook her head slowly and said, "Only you Steve Jirgal. Only you!"

Humor just might be the antidote you need to open your pressure relief valve and ease your stress. Work hard. Fight your way to the top. Take what you do very seriously but remember to enjoy the view as you climb. And don't forget to lighten up a bit. It just might save you from blowing a mental gasket.

The old adage carries great weight, "You only go around once in life, but if you live right, once is enough." There is plenty of room in life's hall of fame. The opportunity and the choice are yours! Find your personal pedestal, climb on top, and enjoy the accolades!

Conclusion

I'm sure you've realized that *Intentional Steps* is an eclectic project. In all likelihood there are some topics that will resonate with you more than others. It's also possible that you know of some people you feel would greatly benefit from reading particular parts contained in this book. It would be to your advantage to camp out on those areas which hit home with you. Furthermore, I would encourage you to share it with those you feel would be helped by particular topics.

But wherever you or others are, *Intentional Steps* might be just what you or they need to go to the next level. Hockey great Wayne Gretsky is quoted as saying, "You miss 100 percent of the shots you never take."

For you and me that means we miss 100% of the opportunities we never take. Today could be the day when you decide to make the changes in your life that will change the direction of your life. Without doubt, it's completely up to you. For all of us, changes must be made, opportunities must be grasped, dreams must be pursued, and mountains must be climbed. But it all starts with the first step!

About the Author

Dr. Jirgal is a 1980 graduate of Gettysburg College where he became a four-time conference champion, All-American, and inductee to the Middle Atlantic Conference *All Century Team* in the pole vault. He holds an undergraduate degree in health education and physical education. Following graduation, he taught on the high school and college level while coaching football and track in both venues. He holds masters degrees in health education, sports medicine, and divinity, as well as a doctorate in ministry.

He has been the director of Sports Medicine at Wingate University, area director for the Fellowship of Christian Athletes and has served on the staff of Hickory Grove Baptist Church in Charlotte, NC, as well as leading Lakeview Baptist Church, in Monroe, NC as the Senior Pastor. He has served on the local board of directors for the Fellowship of Christian Athletes, New Orleans Baptist Seminary and the ministerial board of Wingate University. He currently serves on the board of directors for The Carolina Study Center, and Fathers in Touch ministry.

Dr. Jirgal is the founder and director of *The Jirgal Leadership Institute* where he strives to equip people for success in leadership roles. He and his wife Pam live in Mint Hill, NC and have three grown children, Joshua, Caleb, and Sarah.

BOOKS BY DR. STEVE A. JIRGAL

The Path of a Champion

Dying to Live

Life Points

Principles of Wholeness

Mining the Mind of King Solomon

Laws to Live By

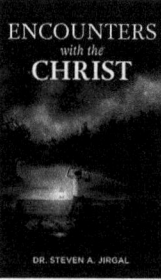
Encounters with the Christ

Intentional Steps

Questions regarding any of these titles can be directed to Jirgalleadership@gmail.com

www.ingramcontent.com/pod-product-compliance
Lightning Source LLC
Chambersburg PA
CBHW051659090426
42736CB00013B/2454